Flo

& WALT D   ...ORLD

GEORGIA

Tallahassee

FLORIDA

Atlantic
Ocean

Gulf of
Mexico

Tampa

Orlando

Miami

Key West

DIAMOND BOOKS

YOUR COLLINS TRAVELLER

Your Collins Traveller Guide will help you find your way around your chosen destination quickly and simply. It is colour-coded for easy reference:

The blue section answers the question 'I would like to see or do something; where do I go and what do I see when I get there?' This section is arranged as an alphabetical list of topics. It is recommended that an up-to-date atlas or street plan is used in conjunction with the location maps in this section. Within each topic you will find:
- A selection of the best examples on offer.
- How to get there, costs and opening times for each entry.
- The outstanding features of each entry.
- A simplified map, with each entry plotted and the nearest landmark or transport access.

The red section is a lively and informative gazetteer. It offers:
- Essential facts about the main places and cultural items.
  What is La Bastille? Who was Michelangelo? Where is Delphi?

The gold section is full of practical and invaluable travel information. It offers:
- Everything you need to know to help you enjoy yourself and get the most out of your time away, from Accommodation through Baby-sitters, Car Hire, Food, Health, Money, Newspapers, Taxis and Telephones to Youth Hostels.

1993 PRICES	Inexpensive	Moderate	Expensive
Attractions			
Museums, etc.	under $5	$5-10	over $10
Restaurants			
Per main course	under $10	$10-20	over $20
Nightclubs			
Entry	under $5	$5-10	over $10

Gatorland Zoo, Orlando

Cross-references:

Type in small capitals – CHURCHES – tells you that more information on an item is available within the topic on churches.

A-Z after an item tells you that more information is available within the gazetteer. Simply look under the appropriate name.

A name in bold – **Holy Cathedral** – also tells you that more information on an item is available in the gazetteer – again simply look up the name.

CONTENTS

CONTENTS

INTRODUCTION

The very name Florida carried the message of warmth and ease and comfort. It was irresistible.' So wrote John Steinbeck over 50 years ago. In his day there were no theme parks and Mickey Mouse was a mere youngster. But what Florida did have going for it then, as it does now, was a marvellous year-round climate, mile upon mile of glorious beaches, and resourceful, hard-working people, determined to make the Sunshine State the world's number one tourist attraction. They have succeeded – nowhere else in the world has the art of tourism been so expertly perfected as here. The choice of theme parks, marine-life parks, wildlife parks, sports, beaches, restaurants, bars and nightlife is bewildering and limited only by your budget. Florida is not cheap, but while it is usually good value, you should beware of the 'hidden extras' – insurance, tips and taxes – when you are planning your trip.

Most tourists head straight for Orlando and Walt Disney World (WDW) even before they have unpacked. Certainly, no one with children should miss the Magic Kingdom. After a few minutes inside the park even the most cynical grown-ups will be queueing to have their picture taken with Mickey or Pluto. It's not a case of having to suspend your disbelief – the real world simply does not exist here. The rest of WDW is also a hugely enjoyable fantasy, and to a large extent this sets the tone for most of central Florida's attractions. Step back into the Wild West, visit Africa, go to the Moon, join King Henry's feast, meet King Kong, see improbable wildlife performing unlikely feats . . . who wants the hassle of going to Africa when Busch Gardens is only 85 miles away? Attraction hosts (visitors are 'guests' in Florida) are frequently super-efficient and most of the time you won't even have to think for yourself. Within the theme worlds you'll never see an overflowing garbage can, litter on the sidewalk, or a burned-out light bulb.

If it all gets a little too slick – even antiseptic – leave Orlando (which has a limited amount to offer above and beyond the theme parks) for the excitement of Florida's other cities and the beauty of its beaches. The illuminated skyscrapers of Miami's skyline are almost as impressive as Epcot's pyrotechnics, and the Art Deco district of Miami Beach is something of a fantasy-land theme park for the trendy. But firmly rooted in reality is the city's crime problem. Tampa cannot compete with

Miami's energy, but it tries, particularly in Ybor City, a fascinating Cuban neighbourhood that was once the world's cigar-making centre. For more sedate sightseeing, head north to atmospheric St. Augustine to explore the country's oldest town, or cross into the Panhandle – more 'Deep South' than Florida – to Tallahassee, the state's backwater capital, and the enchanting historic districts and naval air force museum *sans pareil* of Pensacola.

But after footslogging on the concrete of the theme parks you may just want to chill out on the beach. Your choice of resort is limitless, from the boisterousness of student-orientated Daytona and Panama City Beach to the exclusivity of a luxury hotel complex on Amelia Island in the northeast, or on Sanibel and Captiva on the Lee Island coast. Many resorts, such as Fort Lauderdale on the Atlantic coast and Naples and Sarasota on the Gulf coast, manage to cater for all, with affordable accommodation

and interesting museums for visitors next to swanky shops and country clubs for well-to-do residents.

To the south lie two of America's natural wonders – the great 'sea of grass' wilderness known as the Everglades, and the chain of 32 coral and limestone islands known as the Florida Keys. With the exception of Key West, the USA's very own Caribbean island with Bahamian influences and bohemian people, the keys are quiet, natural and mostly underdeveloped, but have few beaches.

If you get restless from lying on the beach, you can have as sporty a holiday as your body will allow. For example, a tennis court or golf course is never far away, and fishing trips (along with more placid cruises) are part of the entertainment that every resort lays on.

In terms of practical advice, if you can't drive or don't fancy a holiday that involves regular use of a car, think about holidaying elsewhere: a car is essential for virtually any trip in Florida. If you're thinking about exploring the outer reaches of the state, remember that distances are massive. Lastly, Florida is drainingly hot. For sightseers, winter is the best time to visit and is considered high season, particularly in the southern part of the state.

Hemingway House, Key West

Fort Lauderdale

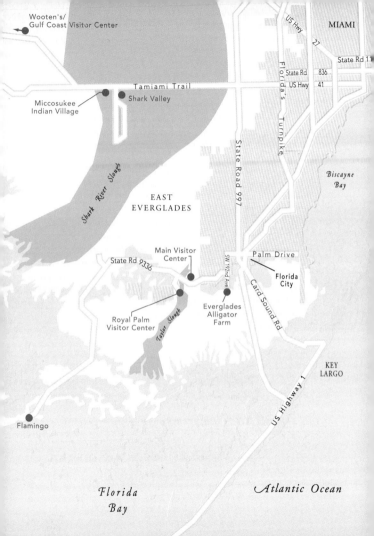

Wooten's/
Gulf Coast Visitor Center

MIAMI

US Hwy 27

State Rd 11

Florida's Turnpike

State Rd 836

US Hwy 41

Tamiami Trail

Miccosukee
Indian Village

Shark Valley

Shark River Slough

EAST
EVERGLADES

State Road 997

Biscayne
Bay

Main Visitor
Center

Palm Drive

State Rd 9336

SW 192nd Ave

Florida
City

Royal Palm
Visitor Center

Taylor Slough

Everglades
Alligator
Farm

Card Sound Rd

KEY
LARGO

US Highway 1

Flamingo

Florida
Bay

Atlantic Ocean

MICCOSUKEE INDIAN VILLAGE 30 miles west of Miami on Tamiami Trail/Highway 41. ■ 0900-1700 (last admission 1630). ● Moderate. *The most commercialized of the Everglades Indian village developments. Craft and cookery demonstrations, alligator wrestling, airboat rides and a small museum. The Miccosukee Restaurant on the main road offers catfish, Indian fry bread, pumpkin bread and beefburgers.*

SHARK VALLEY 29 miles west of Miami off the Tamiami Trail/Highway 41. ■ 0830-1800. ● Inexpensive. ■ Tram tours (booking advisable in winter, tel: 305-2218455) 0830-1800. ● Moderate. *Part of the Everglades National Park, Shark Valley holds one of the best concentrations of wildlife in the whole park; you should see alligators, deer and several species of bird. Along the 15 mile loop, you can either take the 2 hr tram tour, hire a bike or walk. A 50 ft observation tower views the vast wetland at the furthest point.*

EVERGLADES ALLIGATOR FARM 4 miles south of Palm Drive on SW 192nd Ave. ■ 0900-1800 (1900 summer). ● Joint entry for farm and airboat ride, Expensive. *Working alligator farm. Alligator wrestling, snake shows and airboat rides.*

MAIN VISITOR CENTER Just within the entrance to the Everglades National Park on the SR 9336. Tel: 305-2427700. ■ Visitor center 0800-1700. Park open 24 hr. ● Moderate. *From the excellent visitor center, pick up a map showing walking trails off the main road between the center and Flamingo (see **EVERGLADES-ATTRACTIONS 2**). One of the most popular is to Pay-Hay-Okee (Indian for 'grassy waters'), along a boardwalk to an observation tower.*

ROYAL PALM VISITOR CENTER 4 miles beyond the Main Visitor Center. ■ 0800-1615. *Ask about ranger-led walks. There are two 0.5 mile trails from here. Anhinga (named after a black cormorant-like bird common in the park) boardwalk trail features alligators, turtles and heron. The Gumbo-Limbo trail enters a tropical hardwood hammock. The Gumbo-Limbo tree is also known as the 'tourist tree' because in hot weather its bark becomes red and peels off!*

EVERGLADES

FLAMINGO 38 miles from the Main Visitor Center. *This is the only development in the national park. It consists of the Flamingo Lodge Hotel (tel: 305-2532241; booked up in winter for months ahead, rooms usually available on spec in summer), a visitor centre (0800-1700, tel: 305-6953101) and a marina. In winter there are trips in Florida Bay and throughout the year into Whitewater Bay. You can also hire bicycles, skiffs and canoes. There are marked canoe and hiking trails.*

WOOTEN'S West of Ochopee on Tamiami Trail/Highway 41. ■ 0800-1700. ● Alligator farm, Moderate. Airboat rides, Moderate. Swamp buggy rides, Moderate. *The largest of the many centres in the western part of the wetlands. Trips into the Big Cypress National Preserve are available, though tours are scenic and cannot guarantee sightings of wildlife.*

GULF COAST VISITOR CENTER 3 miles south of Tamiami Trail/Highway 41 on Highway 29, south of Everglades City. Tel: 813-6952591. ● Entrance to park, Free. Boat tours, Expensive. *The water-side Everglades National Park centre looks across to the Ten Thousand Islands area of the park. There are 1 hr 45 min Ten Thousand Islands and Mangrove Wilderness boat trips. Canoe hire is also available.*

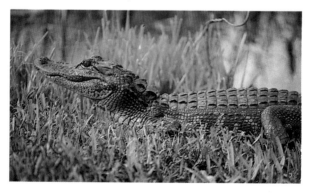

Spaceport USA

Cypress Gardens

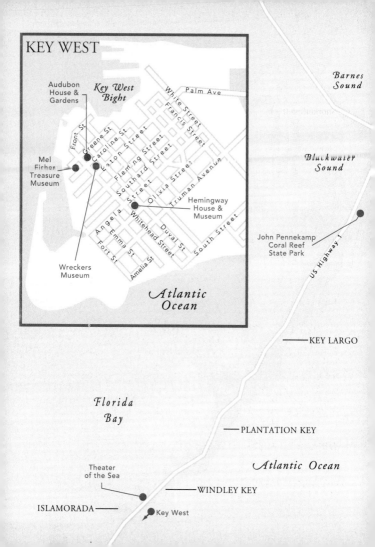

KEY WEST

Audubon House & Gardens

Key West Bight

Palm Ave

White Street

Francis Street

Front St

Greene St

Caroline St

Eaton Street

Fleming Street

Southard Street

Mel Fisher Treasure Museum

Olivia Street

Whitehead Street

Truman Avenue

Hemingway House & Museum

Wreckers Museum

Angela Street

Emma St

Fort St

Duval St

South Street

Amelia St

Atlantic Ocean

Barnes Sound

Blackwater Sound

John Pennekamp Coral Reef State Park

US Highway 1

KEY LARGO

Florida Bay

PLANTATION KEY

Atlantic Ocean

Theater of the Sea

WINDLEY KEY

ISLAMORADA

Key West

Attractions

JOHN PENNEKAMP CORAL REEF STATE PARK
Key Largo, Mile Marker 102.5.
■ 0800-sunset. Glass-bottomed boat trips 0915, 1215 & 1500.
Snorkelling 0900, 1200 & 1500. Scuba diving 0930 & 1330. ● Boat
trip, Moderate. Snorkelling & scuba diving, Expensive. *Board a glass-
bottomed boat for an unforgettable trip to one of Florida's finest reefs.
Stay in the boat, or snorkel or scuba.*

THEATER OF THE SEA Islamorada, Mile Marker 84,
tel: 305-6642431. ■ 0930-1600 (last admission). ● Expensive.
*The main attraction here is swimming with the performing dolphins – if
you have $65. A 90 min tour will introduce you to the Keys' marine life.*

AUDUBON HOUSE & GARDENS Junction of Whitehead St and
Greene St, Key West. ■ 0930-1700. ● Moderate.
*The famous painter and ornithologist J.J. Audubon visited this lovely
19thC house in 1832 and it is now dedicated to him. Audubon
engravings and typical Key West furniture are on display.*

HEMINGWAY HOUSE & MUSEUM Whitehead St, Key West.
■ 0900-1700. ● Moderate.
*Hemingway lived in this elegant but homely Spanish Colonial-style
house from 1931 to 1936, and wrote many famous novels here. See his
study, his beloved cats' descendants, and lots more memorabilia.*

MEL FISHER TREASURE MUSEUM Greene St, Key West.
■ 1000-1700. ● Moderate.
*See remnants from a Spanish galleon lost off the Keys in 1622, including
some of its 47 tonnes of gold and silver treasure. Items on sale from Mel
Fisher's personal collection include silver coins priced at $2.64 million!*

WRECKERS MUSEUM (OLDEST HOUSE) Duval St, Key West.
■ 1000-1600. ● Inexpensive.
*A small museum which is dedicated to the salvage of Keys shipwrecks,
and houses model ships and nautical memorabilia. The building dates
from 1829.*

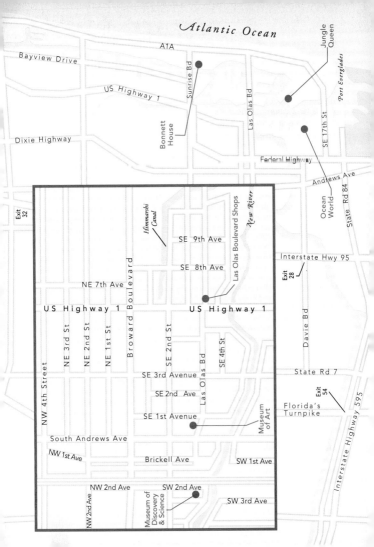

Attractions

BONNETT HOUSE (BARTLETT ESTATES) N Birch Rd.
▦ Guided tours only 1000, 1300 & 1400 Tue.-Fri., 1300 & 1400 Sun. (May-Nov.). ● Moderate.
This is the grandest of the homes in Fort Lauderdale which are open to the public. Built in the 1920s, it features trompe l'oeil marble floors, Moorish décor, an orchid room and period furnishings.

MUSEUM OF DISCOVERY & SCIENCE 401 SW 2nd Ave.
▦ 1000-1700 Mon.-Fri., 1000-2030 Sat., 1200-1700 Sun. ● Moderate.
A new interactive educational museum for all the family.

JUNGLE QUEEN Bahia Mar Yacht Marina, tel: 305-4625596.
▦ Sightseeing cruises 1000 & 1400 (3 hr). ● Moderate. ▦ Dinner cruise 1900 (4 hr). ● Expensive.
By day explore the inland waterways, see Millionaires' Row and stop to see Seminole Indians. By night there is a huge dinner of ribs, chicken and shrimp, then a Vaudeville-style revue. Also cruises to Miami.

LAS OLAS BOULEVARD SHOPS Las Olas Bd, SE 12th Ave and SE 6th Ave. ▦ 1000-1700 Mon.-Sat.
This exclusive shopping street is nationally famous for its jewellery, haute couture clothing, art and antique galleries. Its Spanish-style architecture makes window-shopping a pleasure.

MUSEUM OF ART E Las Olas Bd.
▦ 1100-2100 Tue., 1000-1700 Wed.-Sat., 1200-1700 Sun. Free tours 1300 & 1830 Tue., 1300 Thu. & Fri., 1400 Sat. & Sun. ● Inexpensive.
This ultramodern gallery hosts two excellent collections: north European modern art; and pre-Columbian, West African, Oceanic and American regional and ethnic art.

OCEAN WORLD SE 17th Causeway.
▦ 1000-1800 (last admission 1630). ● Expensive.
The main feature of this small marine-life park is the excellent dolphin and sea lion show. You can also see shark feeding, an exotic birds show, and touch and feed the friendly dolphins.

Fort Lauderdale

CORAL CASTLE South Dixie Highway/Highway 1, Homestead.
■ 0900-1800. ● Moderate.
*This unique and astonishing achievement of coral sculpture and building
by a single man (without the aid of any real machinery) is billed as
'America's Stonehenge'. Huge coral rocking chairs and a 28 tonne
obelisk are some of its wonders.*

MIAMI METROZOO SW 152nd St, South Dade.
■ 0930-1730 (last admission 1600). ● Moderate.
*A 115 hectare cageless zoo where 100 animal species roam, mostly on
moated islands. Star attractions include white tigers, koala bears, a
gorilla and a huge walk-through tropical aviary. A monorail gives a
bird's-eye view of Asian, Eurasian, Australian and African wildlife. There
are daily entertaining, educational shows.*

MONKEY JUNGLE SW 216th St, South Dade.
■ 0930-1800 (last admission 1700). ● Expensive.
*Over 50 species of monkey populate 12 hectares of dense subtropical
jungle. Don't miss Ape Encounter.*

ORCHID JUNGLE SW 157th Ave, Homestead.
■ 0830-1730. ● Moderate.
*The world's largest outdoor orchid garden, featuring over 9000 varieties
of orchid, fern, bromeliad and other rare plants.*

HISTORICAL MUSEUM OF SOUTHERN FLORIDA
Metro-Dade Cultural Center, W Flagler St, Downtown. ■ 1000-1700
Mon.-Sat. (2100 Thu.), 1200-1700 Sun. ● Inexpensive.
*An entertaining look back at the first settlers, Spanish colonialists and
Seminole tribes by means of tableaux, hands-on and audiovisual
exhibits.*

CENTER FOR THE FINE ARTS Metro-Dade Cultural Center,
W Flagler St, Downtown. ■ 1000-1700 Tue.-Sat. (2100 Thu.), 1200-
1700 Sun. ● Moderate.
Hosts large-scale, bi-monthly, top-quality exhibitions.

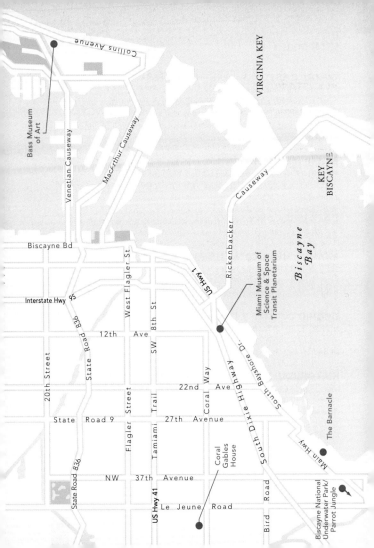

Attractions 2

MIAMI MUSEUM OF SCIENCE & SPACE TRANSIT
PLANETARIUM S Miami Ave, Coconut Grove. ■ 1000-1800.
● Separate entry to museum and planetarium, Moderate.
An educational 'discovery center' with over 150 hands-on exhibits.
There is a small wildlife section dealing with environmental issues.

THE BARNACLE Main Highway, Coconut Grove.
■ 0900-1600 Thu.-Mon. Free tours 1130, 1300 & 1430. ● Inexpensive.
Built in 1886, this peaceful spot was the home of Commodore Ralph
*Munroe, a founder of Coconut Grove (see **Miami**). There are lovely, lush*
grounds.

BASS MUSEUM OF ART Park Ave, Miami Beach.
■ 1000-1700 Tue.-Sat., 1300-1700 Sun. ● Moderate. Tue. donation.
An excellent small exhibition primarily of European art. Works by
Botticelli, Van Dyck and Rubens, plus 16thC Flemish tapestries.

CORAL GABLES HOUSE Coral Way, Coral Gables.
■ 1300-1600 Sun.-Wed. ● Inexpensive.
The boyhood home of George Merrick, founder of Coral Gables (see
Miami*), this lovely house was built in 1899 and enlarged in 1906. See*
MIAMI-EXCURSION.

BISCAYNE NATIONAL UNDERWATER PARK
Tel: 305-2472400. ■ 0730-sunset. ● Free. ■ Cruise 1000. ● Expensive.
■ Snorkelling & scuba trips 1330. ● Expensive.
A glass-bottomed boat goes out to the coral reef, where you can snorkel,
scuba or just stay in the boat. Picnic facilities and canoe rental are also
available.

PARROT JUNGLE SW 57th Ave, South Dade.
■ 0930-1800. ● Expensive.
This beautiful subtropical jungle is the setting for free-flying macaws,
aviaries, flamingos and alligators. Shows on offer include the
unimaginative performing parrots, and the rather more entertaining
flamingo feeding and baby bird training.

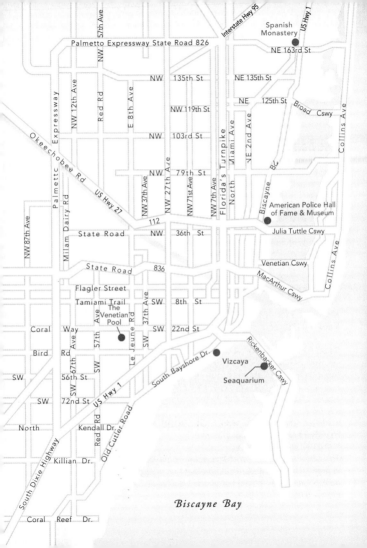

Attractions 3

SEAQUARIUM Rickenbacker Causeway, Key Biscayne.
▦ 0930-1830. ◉ Expensive.
Lolita, the 10,000 lb killer whale, even upstages resident TV star Flipper in the best of several fine shows here. Sea lions, dolphins, sharks, manatees and a large aquarium are the other draws.

SPANISH MONASTERY West Dixie Highway/Highway 1, North Miami Beach.
▦ 1000-1600 Mon.-Sat., 1200-1600 Sun. ◉ Inexpensive.
This ancient building, first erected in Spain in 1141, was brought here by newspaper magnate William Randolph Hearst in 1925. It is now home to a museum of religious art.

THE VENETIAN POOL De Soto Bd, Coral Gables.
▦ 1100-1630 Tue.-Fri., 1000-1630 Sat. & Sun. ◉ Inexpensive.
This beautiful outdoor pool, created in 1924, has rock caves and water-falls. Venetian-inspired architecture surrounds it. See MIAMI-EXCURSION.

VIZCAYA S Miami Ave, Coconut Grove, tel: 305-5792708.
▦ House 0930-1700. Gardens 1000-1730 (last admission 1600).
◉ Moderate.
South Florida's grandest stately home, a magnificent Renaissance-style villa built in 1916, was the winter retreat of industrialist millionaire James Deering. It houses a fine collection of European furnishings, art and décor. Look out for a bed which is said to have belonged to Lady Hamilton, an 18thC ceiling from a Venetian palace, and tapestries once owned by Robert Browning. Grand formal gardens lead to a subtropical jungle area.

AMERICAN POLICE HALL OF FAME & MUSEUM
3801 Biscayne Bd, north of Downtown.
▦ 1000-1730. ◉ Moderate.
Downstairs is a sombre marble memorial to police officers killed when on duty, while upstairs are macabre but fascinating exhibits that you can touch, including an electric chair and a guillotine (neither of which is operational!).

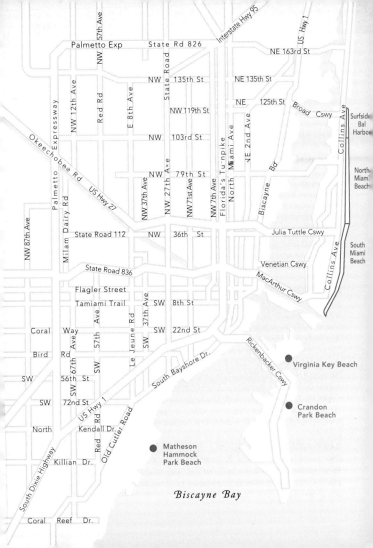

Beaches

MATHESON HAMMOCK PARK BEACH Old Cutler Rd, Coral
Gables. ● Entrance fee.
*Forty hectares of landscaped forest and park conceal a narrow, man-
made, sandy beach which is ideal for small children, as rocks protect it
from the ocean. Lifeguards, swimming pool, boating, nature trail and
picnic area.*

CRANDON PARK BEACH Crandon Park Rd, Key Biscayne.
● Entrance fee.
*Some 200 hectares of wooded parkland open onto 3 miles of wide,
sandy, ocean beach. Picnic, barbecue and playground facilities.*

VIRGINIA KEY BEACH Off Rickenbacker Causeway, Key
Biscayne. ● Entrance fee.
*Similar to other Key Biscayne beaches, but with a more rugged 2 mile-
long sandy beach. Lifeguards are on duty at weekends. Picnic area and
nature trails.*

SOUTH MIAMI BEACH S Pointe Park to 42nd St.
*An Art Deco waterfront is the backdrop for Miami's famous, trendy
beach (known as SoBe), which is always full of life – from models in
G-strings and elderly residents to families and tourists. In the evening
joggers appear and there are soccer tournaments in Lummus Park.
Surfers congregate to the south, and lifeguards are omnipresent.*

NORTH MIAMI BEACH 42nd St (Arthur Godfrey Rd) to 87th St.
*Generally quieter than SoBe. The areas around 46th St and 85th St are
popular with a young crowd. The North Shore State Park from 79th St to
87th St is worth a visit. There are lifeguards and a boardwalk from 21st
St to 46th St.*

SURFSIDE/BAL HARBOR 87th St to 96th St/96th St to 103rd St.
*These beaches are backed by large hotels and condominiums. There are
lifeguards at 93rd St only. North of Bal Harbor is the 2 mile-long
Haulover Park Beach (entrance fee) with picnic, barbecue and play
areas. Beware the strong currents here.*

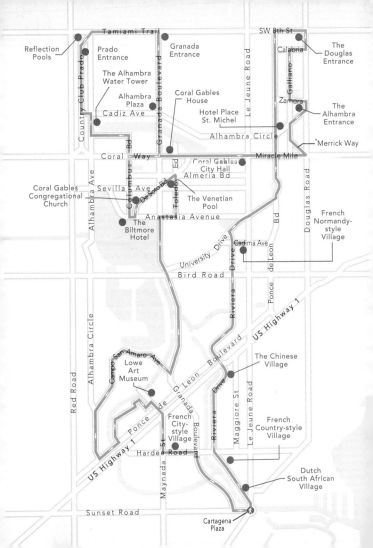

Excursion

A one-day bicycle ride through the old-world ambience of Coral Gables (see **Miami***). The best days to go are Tue. or Wed., when all the shops and attractions are open. The nearest bicycle hire (see* **A-Z***) is at Coconut Grove.*

Start at Cartagena Plaza. Head north on Riviera Drive until you meet Le Jeune Rd.

0.25 mile – Dutch South African Village. One of several 'villages' in the Gables, this was built to resemble the farmhouses of 17thC Dutch colonists. Continue on Riviera Drive.

0.75 mile – French Country-style Village. Another 'village' designed to give this exclusive area even more character. Head north on either Riviera Drive or Maggiore St.

1.5 miles – The Chinese Village. Not easily missed, with its green and yellow pagoda-style roofs. Return to Riviera, and continue across Highway 1 and Ponce de Leon Bd. Turn right at Cadima Ave.

3 miles – French Normandy-style Village. Return to Riviera, turn right onto University Drive, leaving the cycle path, and continue north, joining up with Ponce de Leon Bd. Cross Miracle Mile.

4.5 miles – Hotel Place St. Michel. A charming little European hotel which is full of antiques. Its award-winning restaurant is open daily for lunch (1100-1500) or Sun. brunch (1100-1430). Continue on Ponce de Leon Bd and turn right onto SW 8th St.

5.5 miles – SW 8th St/Calle Ocho. This is the main street of Miami's Little Havana district (see **Miami**). Turn right onto Douglas Rd.

5.75 miles – The Douglas Entrance. This graceful 40 ft arch was built in 1924 as the deliberately awe-inspiring main gateway to Coral Gables. Take a detour via Calabria, Galliano and Zamora before rejoining Douglas Rd.

7 miles – The Alhambra Entrance. Another splendid coral-rock gate-way to the Gables. Join the Alhambra Circle and take Merrick Way.

7.75 miles – Miracle Mile. The Gables' famous shopping street is looking slightly dated but is still worth a spot of window-shopping. The 'Mile' runs into Coral Way, which together with its surrounding streets is one of Miami's loveliest residential areas.

8.5 miles – Coral Gables City Hall. This elegant Spanish Renaissance

edifice was built in 1927. Go inside and see its mural depicting scenes of the area's early days.

9.25 miles – Coral Gables House (see MIAMI-ATTRACTIONS 2). This is the turn-of-the-century family home of George Merrick, the man who founded the Gables. Turn right onto Columbus Bd, left at the golf course, then right onto Alhambra Ave.

10.75 miles – The Alhambra Water Tower. Built in 1924. Turn left onto Country Club Prado and continue to the end of it.

12.25 miles – Prado Entrance & Reflection Pools. Turn right onto the Tamiami Trail and right again at the Granada Entrance to return to Coral Gables, crossing en route the lovely Granada Plaza and golf course. Turn left off Coral Way onto Columbus Bd.

12.75 miles – Coral Gables Congregational Church. This lovely church dates from 1924.

13 miles – The Biltmore Hotel. This is the architectural centrepiece of Coral Gables, recently refurbished at a cost of $38 million. Look inside to admire the lobby and see the 1.25 million-gallon swimming pool (open to the public). Head up De Soto Bd, past the fountain, to the corner of Almeria Bd.

13.5 miles – The Venetian Pool (see MIAMI-ATTRACTIONS 3). This is the perfect place to cool off. Head south down Toledo Bd, turn right onto Anastasia Ave and left onto Granada Bd. Follow Campo San Amaro Ave all the way round the University of Miami campus.

18.25 miles – Lowe Art Museum. This fine collection includes European, Renaissance and Baroque works, plus a collection of indigenous American, Latin and Indian pieces (1000-1700 Tue.-Sat., 1200-1700 Sun.; Inexpensive). Cross back over Ponce de Leon Bd and Highway 1 onto Maynada St, then turn left onto Hardee Rd.

19 miles – French City-style Village. Turn right into Granada Bd and return to Cartagena Plaza.

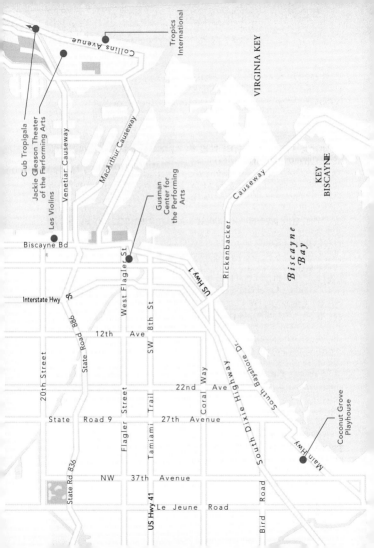

COCONUT GROVE PLAYHOUSE Main Highway, Coconut Grove, tel: 305-4424000. ■ Season Oct.-June.
Nationally acclaimed for a tradition of original productions and Broadway shows, this fine theatre presents regional, national and world premieres.

GUSMAN CENTER FOR THE PERFORMING ARTS E Flagler St, Downtown, tel: 305-3720925. ■ Season Oct.-May.
This beautiful ornate theatre with excellent acoustics stages productions by the Theater of Miami and the Miami City Ballet, and concerts by the New World Symphony and Florida Philharmonic orchestras.

JACKIE GLEASON THEATER OF THE PERFORMING ARTS Washington Ave, South Miami Beach, tel: 305-6737300. ■ Season Nov.-May.
Regular productions of such Broadway favourites as Fiddler on the Roof, Les Miserables *and* Cats *are staged here. Beware some visibility and acoustic difficulties.*

CLUB TROPIGALA Fontainebleau Hilton, Collins Ave, Miami Beach, tel: 800-SHOW. ■ Dinner 1830-0100 (show 2030) Wed., Thu. & Sun., 1830-0300 (shows 2000 & 2200) Fri. & Sat. ● Cover charge, Expensive. Valet parking.
Exotic, tropical dinner/nightclub harking back to the '50s. Two orchestras play Latin and top 40 music, followed by a Las Vegas-style revue.

LES VIOLINS Biscayne Bd, Downtown, tel: 305-3718668. ■ Dinner 1900-0100 Tue.-Thu., 1900-0300 Fri.-Sun. ● Expensive. Valet parking.
Florida's longest-running supper club (established 1965) has a dance band plus two Las Vegas-style revues nightly. Spanish-Cuban menu.

TROPICS INTERNATIONAL Edison Hotel, Ocean Drive, South Miami Beach, tel: 305-5315335. ■ 0800-0200 Sun.-Thu., 0800-0330 Fri. & Sat. ● No cover charge.
A busy nightclub featuring jazz and rhythm-and-blues artists. Sit inside or out by the pool.

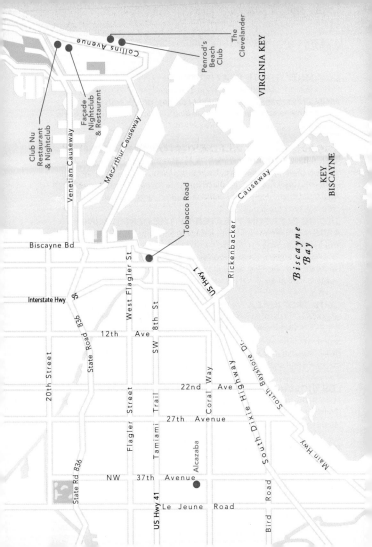

Collins Avenue

The Clevelander

Penrod's Beach Club

VIRGINIA KEY

Club Nu Restaurant & Nightclub

Façade Nightclub & Restaurant

Venetian Causeway

MacArthur Causeway

KEY BISCAYNE

Rickenbacker Causeway

Tobacco Road

Biscayne Bd

Biscayne Bay

Interstate Hwy 95

West Flagler St

US Hwy 1

State Road 836

12th Ave

SW 8th St

20th Street

22nd Ave

Coral Way

South Bashore Dr

27th Avenue

South Dixie Highway

Flagler Street

Tamiami Trail

Alcazaba

NW 37th Avenue

Le Jeune Road

US Hwy 41

Bird Road

Main Hwy

THE CLEVELANDER Ocean Drive, South Miami Beach, tel: 305-5313485. ■ 1200-0300 Sun.-Thu., 1200-0500 Fri. & Sat. ● No cover charge. *This classic Art Deco hotel nightspot regularly pulls in 1500 people on weekend nights. A reggae band plays on Sun. The hotel has several bars, pool tables and backgammon.*

FAÇADE NIGHTCLUB & RESTAURANT NE 163rd St, North Miami Beach, tel: 305-9486868. ■ 2100-0600 Tue.-Sun. ● Cover charge, Moderate-Expensive. Ladies free Wed., Thu. & Sun. *Large dance club/disco with a ten-piece house band, state-of-the-art light and video show, and the Façade Dancers. Dance to top 40 sounds. There is also a gourmet restaurant.*

TOBACCO ROAD 626 S Miami Ave, Downtown, tel: 303-3741198. ■ 1130-1430 Mon.-Fri., 1730-0330 Sun. & Thu., 1730-0500 Fri. & Sat. ● Cover charge, Moderate. *Established in 1912 and a former speakeasy, this rock and blues bar is a Miami institution. Two live bands (one upstairs, one downstairs) play at weekends. The atmosphere is dark, moody and casual.*

PENROD'S BEACH CLUB 1 Ocean Drive, South Miami Beach, tel: 305-5381111. ■ 2100-0300 Sun.-Thu., 2100-0500 Fri. & Sat. Free buffet 1700-2000 Fri. ● Cover charge Moderate. Valet parking. *Rock 'n' roll and dance tunes from the '60s, and live rock and pop bands at the weekend. There is a casual atmosphere, with dancers nightly.*

CLUB NU RESTAURANT & NIGHTCLUB 245 22nd St, South Miami Beach, tel: 305-6720068. ■ 2200-0500 Tue.-Thu., 2200-0900 Fri. & Sat. ● Expensive. *Recently voted one of the world's top 20 night-clubs. Live soul and rock. A club for the extrovert rich and famous.*

ALCAZABA Hyatt Regency Hotel, Alhambra Plaza, Coral Gables, tel: 305-4411234. ■ 1700-0200 Wed. & Fri., 2100-0200 Sat. ● Moderate. *High-energy disco with a Latin flavour – top 40, '70s, '80s, house and salsa music. Black and purple Spanish décor. Ladies' night on Wed.*

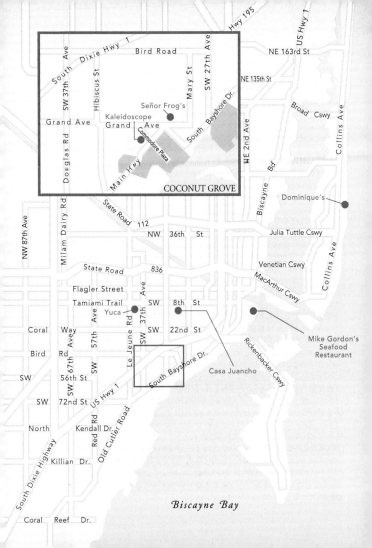

DOMINIQUE'S Alexander Hotel, Collins Ave, North Miami Beach, tel: 305-8655252. ■ 1130-1400, 1800-2330. Sun. brunch in winter. ● Very Expensive. Dress formal. *One of Miami's most beautiful restaurants – galleried, with fittings from old New York mansions – with a garden and ocean views. French nouvelle cuisine is served, but buffalo, alligator and rattlesnake are also on the menu! Some outdoor tables.*

CASA JUANCHO SW 8th St (Calle Ocho), Little Havana, tel: 305-6422452. ■ 1200-2400. ● Expensive. *Excellent Spanish food, including wonderful suckling pig and crema catalana, is served in a setting which could be old Castile. Strolling players move among the tables.*

KALEIDOSCOPE Commodore Plaza, Coconut Grove, tel: 305-4465010. ■ 1130-1500 daily, 1800-2300 Mon.-Thu., 1800-2400 Fri. & Sat. ● Moderate-Expensive. *An intimate restaurant with antique paintings and mirrors, serving excellent Continental and seafood cuisine. A charming balcony looks down onto Coconut Grove (see* **Miami***).*

YUCA Giralda Ave, Coral Gables, tel: 305-4444448. ■ 1200-1600 Mon.-Sat., 1730-2300 Sun.-Thu., 1800-2400 Fri. & Sat. ● Moderate-Expensive. *One of Florida's most talked-about restaurants, combining traditional Cuban food with New American influences (see* **Food***). Highlights include plantain stuffed with cured beef, ribs with spicy guava sauce and paella with linguini instead of rice. Classical décor.*

SEÑOR FROG'S Grand Ave, Coconut Grove. ■ 1130-0100. ● Moderate. *Good-quality, imaginative Mexican dishes are served in a lively garden restaurant. Arrive early to make sure you get an outside seat. Occasionally mariachi (Mexican strolling players) will perform.*

MIKE GORDON'S SEAFOOD RESTAURANT 79th St Causeway, and at Four Ambassadors Hotel, S Bayshore Drive, Coconut Grove. ■ 1200-2200. ● Moderate. Valet parking. *The 79th St original is a low wooden shack with red gingham, nautical décor, and a picture window looking out to the water. The wide selection of fish and seafood specialities is popular with Miamians.*

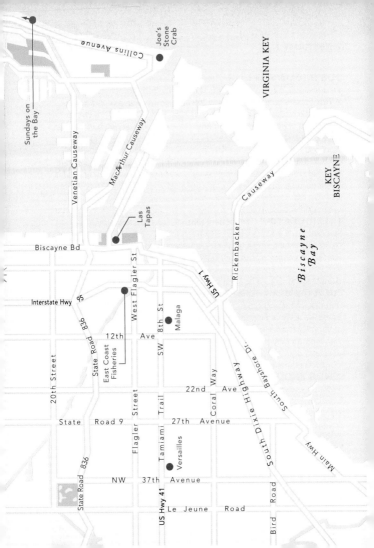

Restaurants 2

JOE'S STONE CRAB Biscayne St, South Miami Beach.
■ 1130-0200 Tue.-Sat., 1700-2200 daily. ● Moderate. No reservations.
*A Florida legend for 77 years, the 'obligatory' meal here is stone crab
claws with mustard sauce, creamed garlic spinach and hash browns,
followed by Key lime pie. Go at lunch or early evening to avoid queues.*

EAST COAST FISHERIES Flagler St, Downtown. ■ 1130-2230.
● Moderate. *Over 40 types of fish are served in this dockside favourite
which doubles as a fish market. Sit upstairs to see your meal prepared in
the open kitchen.*

LAS TAPAS Bayside Marketplace entrance. ■ 1130-2400 Mon.-Thu.
& Sun., 1130-0100 Fri. & Sat. ● Moderate. *Large, authentic, smart
Spanish restaurant complete with dozens of cured hams hanging from
the ceiling. Good choice of* tapas *(small lunch/appetizer dishes) and
interesting entrées. There are tables outside.*

SUNDAYS ON THE BAY Crandon Bd, Key Biscayne, & Collins
Ave, Haulover. ■ 1130-1630, 1730-2400 Mon.-Thu., 1130-0045 Fri.-
Sun. ● Moderate. *The big attractions here are the water and the* Miami
Vice-*style speedboats that draw up outside. Relaxed and friendly, the
menu is seafood-orientated but people come here as much for a drink or
to listen to the reggae and jazz as for the food.*

MALAGA SW 8th St (Calle Ocho), Little Havana. ■ 1130-2330.
● Moderate. ■ El Tablao shows 2130 & 2330 Mon. & Wed.-Sat., plus
0100 Fri. & Sat. ● Expensive. *Generous portions of Cuban and Spanish
home-style cooking (see* **Food***) are served in a casual Latin atmosphere.
Try the* paella Valenciana. *The El Tablao flamenco show is in an
adjoining room.*

VERSAILLES SW 8th St (Calle Ocho), Little Havana. ■ 0800-0200
Sun.-Thu., 0800-0330 Fri., 0800-0430 Sat. ● Inexpensive. *Miami's
quintessential Cuban restaurant. Basic décor but great-value food, such
as Cuban classics* arroz con pollo *(see* **Food***),* palomilla *(a flat steak), and
vieja ropa (shredded beef in a tomato sauce). Very popular late on.*

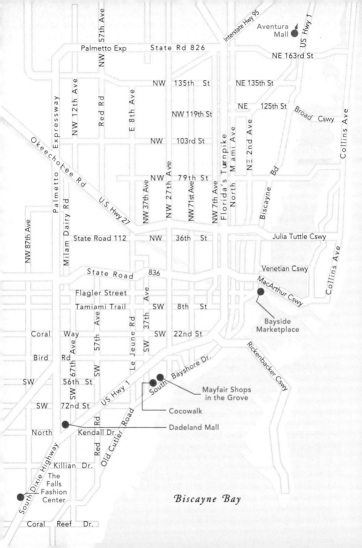

Shopping

AVENTURA MALL Biscayne Bd, North Miami Beach.
▦ 1000-2130 Mon.-Sat., 1100-1800 Sun.
Miami's largest indoor mall comprises over 200 shops and 21 eating places, anchored by the famous department stores Sears, Macy's and J.C. Penney.

BAYSIDE MARKETPLACE Biscayne Bd, Downtown.
▦ 1000-2200 Mon.-Sat., 1200-2000 Sun. (some shops open later).
This vibrant, bayfront, Covent Garden-style centre offers an excellent selection of high-quality arts, crafts and fashion clothing at reasonable prices. The perfect place for souvenirs and presents. See **Miami***.*

COCOWALK 3015 Grand Ave, Coconut Grove.
▦ 1100-2200 Sun.-Thu., 1100-2400 Fri. & Sat.
'Fashion! Food! Fun!' broadcasts the sign outside. Popular bars and restaurants, improvisation comedy and a cinema are situated above mainstream clothes shops such as The Gap.

DADELAND MALL N Kendall Drive, Kendall.
▦ 1000-2100 Mon.-Sat., 1200-1730 Sun.
Over 185 speciality stores plus five department stores make this Miami's most comprehensive 'serious shopping' mall. There's a good choice of places to eat and it's adjacent to Dadeland North Metrorail (see **Miami***).*

THE FALLS FASHION CENTER Howard Drive (Highway 1/SW 136th St), Kendall. ▦ 1000-2100 Mon.-Sat., 1200-1700 Sun.
This relatively small centre includes Miami's only Bloomingdale's. It is set around a lovely open-air watercourse of gentle falls, pools and lush greenery linked by boardwalks and bridges.

MAYFAIR SHOPS IN THE GROVE Grand Ave, Coconut Grove.
▦ 1000-2000 Mon. & Thu., 1000-1900 Tue., Wed., Fri. & Sat., 1200-1730 Sun.
Miami's most beautiful mall. Inside, exotic tiles, sculptures and cascading fountains; outside, a riot of bougainvillea. High-fashion exclusive names include Charles Jourdan, Yves St. Laurent and Ralph Lauren.

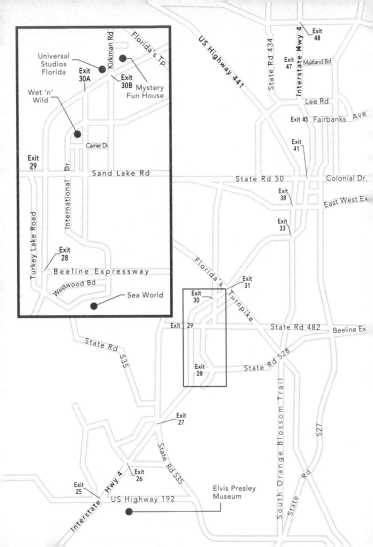

Attractions 1

UNIVERSAL STUDIOS FLORIDA 1000 Universal Studios Plaza, tel: 407-3638000. ■ Open 0900. Closing times vary according to the season. ● $37.10, child 3-9 $29.68, car parking $5. Two-day pass available.
Universal Studios Florida has combined its 75 years of movie-making and studio tour experience with the skills of its creative consultant, Steven Spielberg, to produce an extravaganza of film- and TV-based entertainment and thrills from its most famous productions, including E.T., Jaws and Back to the Future. Don't miss it. See **A-Z**.

MYSTERY FUN HOUSE Major Bd. ■ 1000-2200. ● Moderate. Additional Moderate charge for Starbase Omega.
An old-style fun house for kids, with 15 zany rooms containing mazes, mirrors, a chamber of horrors, etc. Starbase Omega is a laser battle game played in a simulated low-gravity atmosphere.

ELVIS PRESLEY MUSEUM Old Town, Highway 192, Kissimmee. ■ 1000-2300. ● Inexpensive.
This museum claims the largest Elvis collection outside Graceland, with furniture, cars, clothes and gold discs.

WET 'N' WILD International Drive, tel: 407-351-WILD. ■ 1000-1700 Nov.-Mar., ranging from 1000-1800 to 0900-2300 April-Oct. ● $20.95, child 3-12 $18.95. Discounts after 1500 or 1700 depending on the season.
The nation's most popular water park has recently introduced Bomb Bay, an almost vertical 76 ft free fall. Surf Lagoon delivers 4 ft-high body-surfing waves, and assorted flumes will have you spiralling through the waters. Great family fun.

SEA WORLD Sea World Drive, tel: 407-3513600. ■ 0900-2000. Extended hours in high season. ● $32.95, child 3-9 $28.95. Discount combination ticket available with Cypress Gardens (see **ORLANDO-ATTRACTIONS 3**) and Busch Gardens (see **TAMPA-ATTRACTIONS**). *Florida's biggest marine-life park stages exciting shows featuring whales, sea lions, dolphins and starring Shamu, its 6000 lb killer whale. See* **A-Z**.

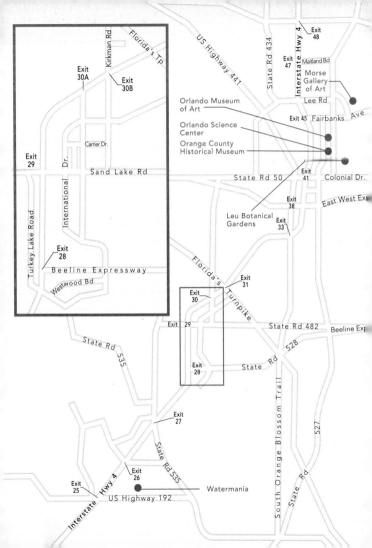

ORLANDO SCIENCE CENTER 810 E Rollins St, tel: 409-8967151. ◼ 0900-1700 Mon.-Thu., 0900-2100 Fri., 1200-2100 Sat., 1200-1700 Sun. ● Moderate. ◼ Planetarium 1400. ● Moderate.
Some 30 hands-on exhibits, as well as a planetarium, to prove that scientific principles can be demonstrated in an entertaining, informative and accessible way. Laser and rock music shows on Fri. & Sat. evenings.

ORANGE COUNTY HISTORICAL MUSEUM 812 E Rollins St. ◼ 0900-1700 Mon.-Sat., 1200-1700 Sun. ● Inexpensive.
Fine creative displays tell the story of Orange County (central Florida) from pioneer days. Room reconstructions include an old general store, a Victorian parlour, a hotel lobby and a 1926 fire depot.

ORLANDO MUSEUM OF ART N Mills Ave. ◼ 0900-1700 Tue.-Sat., 1200-1700 Sun. ● Inexpensive.
Small but interesting display of pre-Columbian (pre-1492) South American art. Temporary exhibitions of modern American art are also featured.

LEU BOTANICAL GARDENS N Forest Ave. ◼ 0900-1700. ● Inexpensive.
Some 22 hectares of peaceful gardens featuring camellias, roses, orchids and a floral clock. Leu House is a restored turn-of-the-century mansion with artefacts dating from 1910 to 1930.

MORSE GALLERY OF ART E Welbourne Ave, Winter Park. ◼ 0930-1600 Tue.-Sat., 1300-1600 Sun. ● Inexpensive.
This beautiful Art Nouveau collection features Tiffany glass, paintings, pottery, metalwork and furniture. Works by contemporary American artists complete the period feel.

WATERMANIA Highway 192, Kissimmee, tel: 407-3962626. ◼ 0930-2000 summer, 1000-1700 spring & autumn. ● Expensive.
Wet features include a wave pool, a 72 ft-high free-fall slide, toboggan chutes and assorted flumes. If you want to keep dry there's a maze, mini-golf and a sandy beach.

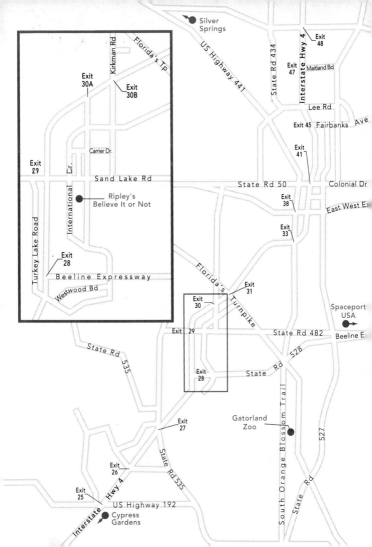

GATORLAND ZOO South Orange Blossom Trail/Highway 17-92-441. ■ 0800-dusk. ● Moderate.
Boardwalks cross the habitats of over 5000 alligators, ranging in size from 8 in to 15 ft. The Jumparoo feeding show is entertaining, and a farm unit and small zoo can also be visited.

CYPRESS GARDENS S Lake Summit Drive, off Highway 27, tel: 813-3242111. ■ 0900-1730. Extended hours in high season. ● $24.30, child 3-9 $17.40. Discount combination ticket available with Sea World (see **ORLANDO-ATTRACTIONS 1**) and Busch Gardens (see **TAMPA-ATTRACTIONS**).
*Florida's longest-running attraction covers over 80 hectares of perfectly manicured lakeside grounds. Famous for its marvellous water-ski show and zoological and botanical gardens. See **A-Z**.*

RIPLEY'S BELIEVE IT OR NOT 8201 International Drive. ■ 1000-2300. ● Moderate.
This is one of a country-wide chain of museums that celebrate the weird and the wonderful. The building itself stands askew. Its contents range from a Rolls Royce which is made of a million matchsticks to the world's largest tyre.

Major attractions within easy reach of Orlando:

SPACEPORT USA (NASA KENNEDY SPACE CENTER)
NASA Parkway (SR 405), near Cocoa Beach, 45 miles east of Orlando. ■ 0800-dusk June-Aug., 0900-dusk Sep.-May. ● Free general admission to site.
*This is a fully operational base and the home of the Space Shuttle. A public show area charts the history and likely future of space exploration and includes a large 'rocket parking lot'. See **A-Z**.*

SILVER SPRINGS 5636 E Silver Springs Bd, Silver Springs, Ocala, 72 miles from Orlando. ■ 0900-1730. ● $19.95, child 3-10 $14.95.
Glass-bottomed boats sail through a tropical landscape stocked with exotic animals. This location was used in the making of the Tarzan films.

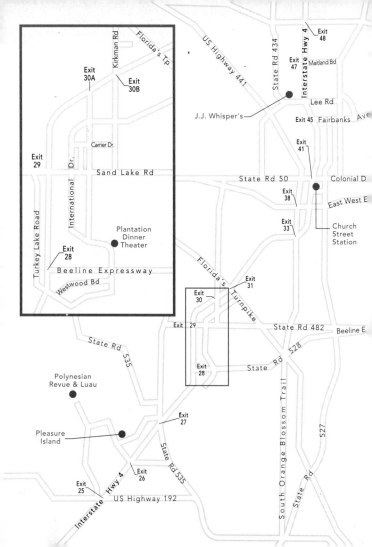

CHURCH STREET STATION Church St.

■ Shows & music 1930-0200. ● $15.95, child 4-12 $9.95. Free admission to shops and restaurants.

This amazing complex was once a crumbling hotel and railroad depot, but it has been brilliantly converted into saloons, bar rooms, restaurants and shops, ranging in style from the 1890s to the roaring '20s, which are fitted out to the highest standards. It stages 20 live shows per night. Choose from two Old West saloons (featuring country and western and Dixieland jazz), a Victorian 'Crystal Palace' with music from the '50s to the '90s, a folk music courtyard and state-of-the-art disco. It's best to eat at Cracker's rather than the overpriced Lili Marlene's. Don't miss the lovely shops (see ORLANDO-SHOPPING).

J.J. WHISPER'S Adanson St/Lee Rd. Tel: 407-6294779 for details of what's on. ■ 1900-0200 Mon.-Sat. ● Moderate.

Orlando's top nightclub features high-energy dancing, top 40 bands, pool rooms, cocktail lounge, restaurant and comedy club.

PLANTATION DINNER THEATER International Drive, tel: 407-3620008. ■ 1700-2200 Tue.-Sat. ● Expensive.

A Broadway-style production is played in the atmospheric Victorian surroundings of this Old South-themed restaurant. The Southern cooking here is probably the best of all of Orlando's dinner shows.

PLEASURE ISLAND Disney Village, Walt Disney World.

■ Times vary. ● $13.95.

*Disney's 'nightlife theme park' includes discos, live music, a comedy club and themed bars. There is free admission to the adjacent restaurants and 'first-run' cinema. See **Walt Disney World**.*

POLYNESIAN REVUE & LUAU Polynesian Village, Walt Disney World, tel: 407-9347639. ■ 1845 & 2130. Reservations required.

● $31, junior 12-20 $24, child 3-11 $16.

The best of the luaus (Hawaiian feasts) on offer, featuring Hawaii-trained dancers, twangy guitars, hypnotic war-drums, and fire-jugglers. Great family evening entertainment.

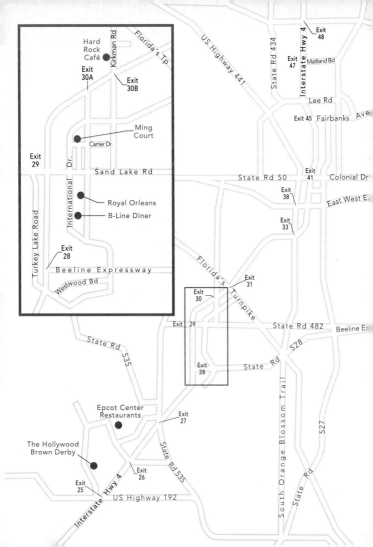

Restaurants

ROYAL ORLEANS Mercado Mediterranean Village, International Drive, tel: 407-3528200. ▪ 1100-1500 Mon.-Fri., 1700-2300 daily. ● Moderate-Expensive. *Excellent Cajun food (see **Food**) in an elegant setting. Choose the* truit roulée *starter and a spice-blackened entrée from the award-winning menu.*

MING COURT International Drive. ▪ 1100-2300. ● Moderate-Expensive. *Large, attractive restaurant with several rooms featuring plum-coloured décor and carved chandeliers. Generous portions of well-presented, tasty Chinese food, including Hunan specialities.*

THE HOLLYWOOD BROWN DERBY Disney/MGM Studios. ▪ Lunch & dinner. Last booking/order 1 hr before park closes. ● Moderate-Expensive. *An atmospheric replica of the world-famous 1929 Hollywood restaurant. Film buffs will love the Wall of Fame autographed caricatures.*

EPCOT CENTER RESTAURANTS Walt Disney World. ▪ Lunch & dinner. Last booking/order 1 hr before park closes. ● Moderate-Expensive. *High-quality restaurants in each of the countries' showcases. At Coral Reef (Living Seas) you can look at the reef while tucking into its inhabitants! Singing waiters (evenings only) at L'Originale Alfredo di Roma Ristorante (Italy) give this elegant place a lively atmosphere. Couscous and tagines are on the easy-to-understand menu at Marrakesh (Morocco), and you can enjoy tempura (deep-fried foods) at Mitsukoshi (Japan). It is permanently 'dusk' at the San Angel Inn (Mexico), and Cap'n Jack's Oyster Bar (Disney Village Marketplace) is ideal for lunch.*

HARD ROCK CAFÉ Universal Studios Florida, 5800 Kirkman Rd, tel: 407-3517625. ▪ 1100-0200. ● Inexpensive-Moderate. *The largest outlet in this world-famous restaurant chain, renowned for its fine burgers, rock 'n' roll memorabilia and great atmosphere.*

B-LINE DINER The Peabody Hotel, International Drive. ▪ Open 24 hr. ● Inexpensive-Moderate. *There's superb '50s-style décor in this smart diner. Quality food and service.*

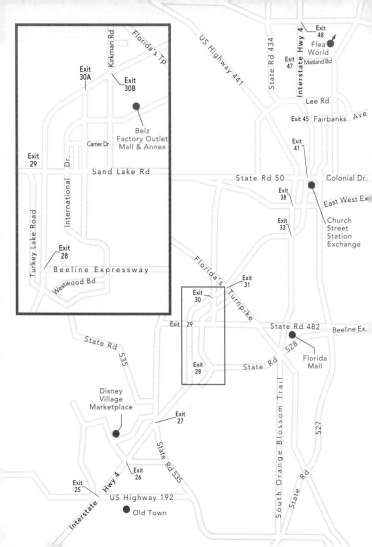

Shopping

CHURCH STREET STATION EXCHANGE Church St.
▨ 1100-2300.
The liveliest shopping in town, featuring over 60 speciality shops and restaurants set in a splendid Victorian-style pavilion. Don't miss the beautiful Bumby Arcade and the Buffalo Trading Company. See
ORLANDO-NIGHTLIFE.

FLORIDA MALL Sand Lake Rd/South Orange Blossom Trail.
▨ 1000-2130 Mon.-Sat., 1100-1800 Sun.
Mediterranean, Victorian and Art Deco architectural themes mix in this massive mall which has over 160 shops and restaurants.

BELZ FACTORY OUTLET MALL & ANNEX W Oak Ridge Rd.
▨ 1000-2100 Mon.-Sat., 1000-1800 Sun.
Savings from 25% to 75% off the retail price of branded goods are possible here at Orlando's biggest discount mall. Some 90 outlets sell clothing, toys, jewellery, records and lots more.

FLEA WORLD Highway 17-92-441, Sanford.
▨ 0800-1700 Fri.-Sun. ● Zoo admission, Inexpensive.
This is claimed to be America's largest regular flea market, holding some 1500 indoor and outdoor stalls dealing in antiques, arts and crafts, clothing, etc. If the kids get bored there's a zoo with 300 animals.

OLD TOWN Highway 192, Kissimmee.
▨ 1000-2200. Restaurants and bars stay open later.
An old-time boulevard of some 70 small speciality shops, restaurants and bars. Lively entertainment is provided by buskers and there's also a large Ferris wheel.

DISNEY VILLAGE MARKETPLACE Walt Disney World.
▨ Shops open 1000-2200.
This pleasant, open-air, lakeside complex is the best place to get your Disney souvenirs. Don't miss Mickey's Character Shop, The Great Southern Country Craft Co., Gourmet Pantry and (at Pleasure Island) YesterEars.

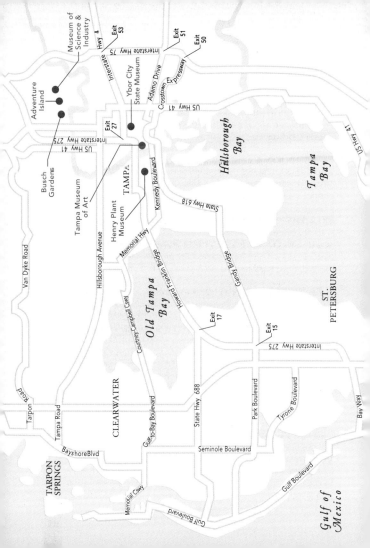

Attractions

BUSCH GARDENS Busch Bd/40th St, tel: 813-9875171.
■ 0930-1800. Extended hours in summer and some hols. ● $27.95,
child 3-9 $22.95, car park $3. *Tampa's top attraction. A free-roaming
zoo park with six exciting roller coaster and water rides, and various live
entertainments, all with an African theme. As stylish a theme park as
anything Orlando can offer.* See **A-Z**.

ADVENTURE ISLAND 4500 Bougainvillea Ave, 0.25 mile northeast of Busch Gardens, tel: 813-9875171. ■ 1000-1700 Mar.-Aug.,
weekends Sep. & Oct. Extended hours in summer and some hols.
● $16.95, child 3-9 $14.95. Three-day pass for Busch Gardens and
Adventure Island $44.95. *First-rate water theme park with exciting rides,
a volleyball complex and imaginative play areas for younger children.*

MUSEUM OF SCIENCE & INDUSTRY (MOSI) 4801 E Fowler
Ave, tel: 813-9855531. ■ 0900-1630 Mon.-Thu. & Sun., 0900-2100
Fri. & Sat. Extended hours in peak seasons. ● Moderate. *An unflashy,
large 'scientific playground'. Interactive exhibits include a space learning
centre, a TV news desk and a hurricane simulator. The museum is
particularly appealing for older children. Undergoing a major expansion.*

TAMPA MUSEUM OF ART 601 Doyle Carlton Drive, tel: 813-
2238130. ■ 1000-1700 Tue. & Thu.-Sat., 1000-2100 Wed., 1300-1700
Sun. ● Inexpensive. *A modern gallery running continuous contemporary
art exhibitions alongside a permanent Classical collection.*

HENRY PLANT MUSEUM University of Tampa, 401 Kennedy Bd,
tel: 813-2541891. ■ 1000-1600 Tue.-Sat. ● Donation. *The Tampa Bay
Hotel, built in 1891, now part of the University of Tampa, was a rich
man's folly. The building's silver minarets and domes impress more than
the small museum itself (a collection of the hotel's antiques).*

YBOR CITY STATE MUSEUM 1818 9th Ave, tel: 813-2476326.
■ 0900-1200, 1300-1700 Tue.-Sat. ● Inexpensive. *A history of the
birth, rise and fall of this unique Cuban neighbourhood, with exhibits on
the cigar industry. Also see the reconstructed cigar-worker's home.*

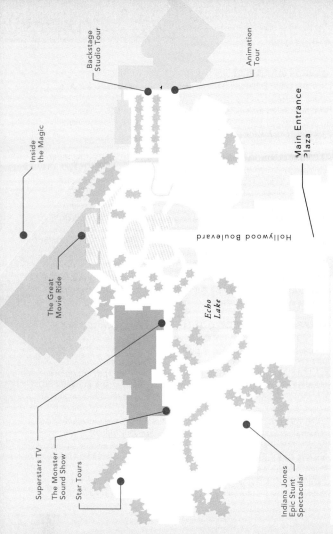

Backstage
Studio Tour

Animation
Tour

Inside
the Magic

Main Entrance
Plaza

Hollywood Boulevard

The Great
Movie Ride

Echo
Lake

Superstars TV

The Monster
Sound Show

Star Tours

Indiana Jones
Epic Stunt
Spectacular

DISNEY/MGM STUDIOS THEME PARK

Disney/MGM Theme Park

■ *0900-1900. Hours extended to 2200 in hols.* ● *One-day ticket $34, child 3-9 $27, car parking $5. For four- and five-day passes, see* **A-Z**.

BACKSTAGE STUDIO TOUR Continuous tours (30 min).
An informative tram tour of the Production Center, which is worth it for Catastrophe Canyon alone. Don't miss it.

ANIMATION TOUR Continuous tours (1 hr). *See an amusing Robin Williams film on the principles of animation then watch artists at work in the studio. Finally, a film montage of unforgettable Disney scenes will have you reaching for the tissues!*

THE GREAT MOVIE RIDE Continuous (5 min). *A ride through classic scenes from Hollywood. Some of the sequences work well, but others (notably* Casablanca) *are best left to the memory.*

INDIANA JONES EPIC STUNT SPECTACULAR 8-10 shows daily (45 min). *An action-packed live production of favourite stunt scenes from* Raiders of the Lost Ark *and* Temple of Doom *is staged on three huge film sets. Great fun.*

THE MONSTER SOUND SHOW Continuous shows (25 min). *Audience members help technicians dub sound effects to a haunted house mystery. The final version is predictably funny.*

STAR TOURS Ride (2 min). *This* Star Wars *simulator thrill ride takes you into the cockpit of Luke Skywalker's spaceship on his hair-raising flight into the Death Star. Highly recommended.*

SUPERSTARS TV Continuous shows (25 min). *Members of the audience are filmed live on stage sets which are then superimposed onto actual footage of such TV favourites as* Cheers! *The end results are frequently hilarious.*

INSIDE THE MAGIC Continuous tours (1 hr). *The tricks of film-making. Water-effects tank, special effects, sound and editing studios.*

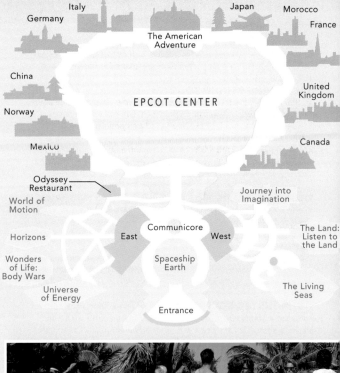

Germany
Italy
Japan
Morocco
France

The American
Adventure

China

United
Kingdom

EPCOT CENTER

Norway

Canada

Mexico

Odyssey
Restaurant

Journey into
Imagination

World of
Motion

Communicore

The Land:
Listen to
the Land

Horizons

East   West

Wonders
of Life:
Body Wars

Spaceship
Earth

The Living
Seas

Universe
of Energy

Entrance

Epcot Future World

■ *0900-2000. Extended hours in summer and hols. Tel: 407-8244321.*
● *One-day ticket $34, child 3-9 $27, car parking $5. For four- and five-day tickets, see A-Z.*

SPACESHIP EARTH *A 5 min journey from early man to the 20thC, taking in the works of ancient Egypt, Rome, Greece, Renaissance Italy, etc. en route. The trip is unexciting but always popular.*

UNIVERSE OF ENERGY *Three films and a clever moving theatre ride take you through 'the forces that fuel our lives', from Animatronic dinosaurs to a thunderous Space Shuttle launch, on a 220° screen.*

WONDERS OF LIFE: BODY WARS *A simulator thrill ride that takes you into the body on a (literally) heart-pounding journey through the bloodstream into the lungs, brain and so on. The ride is confusing but exciting!*

HORIZONS *A ride through the inventions of yesteryear and some fanciful notions of how the future was viewed, is updated to how we now think people will live in years to come. Reasonably entertaining.*

WORLD OF MOTION *A whimsical ride through the history of transport finishes with a brief speed simulator. You then pass to the interesting Transcenter area to see some of the very latest developments.*

JOURNEY INTO IMAGINATION *If time is short, skip the ride, which is rather baffling, but don't miss Captain EO, a 17 min George Lucas film starring Michael Jackson, with incredible 3-D effects.*

THE LAND: LISTEN TO THE LAND *Cruise through various world climes to see how agriculture will look in the future. This educational ride is popular with a slightly older crowd. Fine restaurant.*

THE LIVING SEAS *The Caribbean Coral Reef ride is great for a study of marine life close up. The centrepiece is the world's largest man-made saltwater tank, with over 80 species of tropical fish and mammals.*

Geosphere, Epcot Center

Epcot World Showcase

Opening times and admission costs as **WDW-EPCOT FUTURE WORLD**.

MEXICO *Inside the Mayan pyramid it is 'outdoors', dusk, the cicadas are chirping, both street market and restaurant-hacienda are bustling, and in the distance a volcano erupts. The boat ride is pleasant but it is not a 'must'.*

NORWAY *The main attraction here is the (rather disappointing) Viking boat ride through fjords, past trolls and – back to the future – a huge oil rig. The film that follows is very poor. If the queues are long, miss both and see the rest of the pavilion.*

CHINA *One of the highlights of Epcot, this beautiful pavilion features exotic buildings, some exquisite art exhibits and one of the best Circlevision films in Walt Disney World.*

THE AMERICAN ADVENTURE *The main event is a 30 min Audio-Animatronics show relating the development of the US. Figures such as a walking, talking Benjamin Franklin are impressive but unless you are a US patriot you may find it a little boring.*

JAPAN *The serenity of this lovely enclave, which includes a gallery of traditional and contemporary art, contrasts with the bustle of the large, fascinating Mitsukoshi department store. Be sure to see the drumming and dancing outside the pagoda.*

MOROCCO *A prayer tower from Marrakesh, a gateway from Fez and some 9 tonnes of hand-crafted tiles make this one of Epcot's architectural delights. Don't miss the small museum or the palatial restaurant.*

FRANCE *Beautiful shops, an irresistible boulangerie/patisserie and the Eiffel Tower create a je ne sais quoi Gallic atmosphere. Don't miss an excellent half-Circlevision film.*

CANADA *The vast natural beauty of Canada lends itself perfectly to the panoramic sweep of Circlevision.*

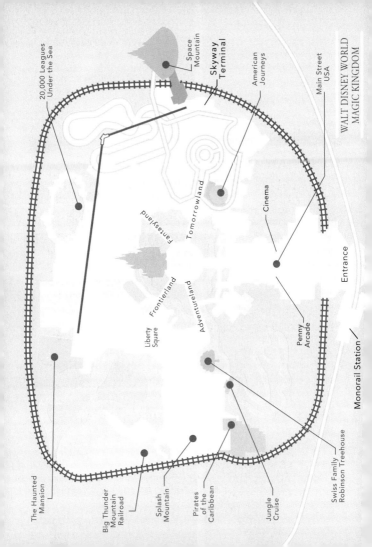

WALT DISNEY WORLD
MAGIC KINGDOM

Space Mountain

Skyway Terminal

American Journeys

Main Street USA

20,000 Leagues Under the Sea

Cinema

Tomorrowland

Fantasyland

Frontierland

Liberty Square

Adventureland

Entrance

Penny Arcade

Monorail Station

The Haunted Mansion

Big Thunder Mountain Railroad

Splash Mountain

Pirates of the Caribbean

Jungle Cruise

Swiss Family Robinson Treehouse

Magic Kingdom

▦ *From 0900-1900 off season to 0900-2400 in summer and peak hols.*
Tel: 407-8244321. ◉ *One-day ticket $34, child 3-9 $27, car parking $5.*
For 4- and 5-day passes, see **A-Z**. *Entries listed based on clockwise tour.*

MAIN STREET USA
A magical re-creation of an idealized turn-of-the-century small American
Main Street. The attraction here is mostly shopping, but don't miss the
Penny Arcade or the small cinema (continuous shows).

SWISS FAMILY ROBINSON TREEHOUSE Adventureland.
This huge man-made banyan is the perfect treehouse, with (nearly) every
comfort, including running water.

JUNGLE CRUISE Adventureland.
A gentle 10 min boat trip through waterfalls, jungles, the Nile valley and
the African veld encountering elephants, lions, giraffes, hippos and
head-hunters. Good effects and commentary.

PIRATES OF THE CARIBBEAN Adventureland.
You can't fail to be impressed as your boat suddenly emerges from its tunnel into the crossfire of a port being bombarded by a life-sized pirate ship. Float on through the village to see the drunken raid. This is Disney Animatronics at their best.

SPLASH MOUNTAIN Frontierland.
A railroad ride that culminates in an exhilarating 40 mph flume drop. Expect long queues.

BIG THUNDER MOUNTAIN RAILROAD Frontierland.
A relatively tame 3 min roller-coaster runaway train ride, speeding through old mining tunnels and a gold diggers' settlement. There are some good Animatronics in and around the 200 ft-high mountain.

THE HAUNTED MANSION Liberty Square.
Frightening it isn't, but this ghost train ride has lots of good special effects – especially when a ghost gets in your car – and children will love it.

20,000 LEAGUES UNDER THE SEA Fantasyland.
Five feet under the lagoon to be precise! The fake sea creatures are, by Disney standards, awful, but the submarine illusion is convincing and it's worth doing if the queue isn't too long.

AMERICAN JOURNEYS Tomorrowland.
The fastest and cheapest way of seeing America coast-to-coast, by plane, helicopter, boat and train, courtesy of Circlevision.

SPACE MOUNTAIN Tomorrowland.
Disney World's only white-knuckle ride sends you hurtling into the darkness at 30 mph, but the out-of-control speed sensation is double that. Thrilling by anyone's standards!

FORT WILDERNESS
■ Free.
Essentially a WDW camping and caravanning resort, this 240 hectare forested area has lots for non-WDW guests to do as well, from hiring bikes, boats and canoes to horse-riding (tel: 407-8242900), fishing (no licence required) and water sports. The area is perfect for walks and picnics, and there is a small-animals farm.

DISCOVERY ISLAND Fort Wilderness.
■ 1000-dusk. ● $8.50, child 3-9 $4.75. Discount combination ticket available with River Country (see below) $16.75, child 3-9 $12.25.
The perfect antidote to the crowds and Audio-Animatronics, this lovely wildlife island features parrots, monkeys, vultures, flamingos, alligators and giant tortoises in natural habitats.

RIVER COUNTRY
Tel: 407-8244321. ■ 0900-2000 summer, 0900-1800 winter.
● $13.25, child 3-9 $10.50. Discount combination ticket available with Discovery Island (see above) $16.75, child 3-9 $12.25.
This water-playground comprises a huge landscaped swimming pool and a walled-off area of the lake where there are flumes, a rapids ride, swings and diving platforms. There's also a lovely white-sand beach and picnic facilities.

TYPHOON LAGOON
Tel: 407-8244321. ■ 1000-1700 out of season, 0900-2000 summer and hols. ● $20.55, child $16.50.
This is probably the world's most innovative water-theme park. It features an 85 ft-high mountain spewing out nine waterslides, the world's largest inland surfing lagoon for body- and inflatable-raft surfing, and a Caribbean reef for snorkelling, complete with its own sharks (behind secure Plexiglas!). Tropical landscaping and a white-sand beach complete the fantasy. Picnics are permitted.

St. Petersburg

Amelia Island: 168 miles north of Orlando. The island, named after George II's daughter, was occupied from 1562 by the French, Spanish, English and Mexicans, before being ceded to the US in 1821. Exclusive resort hotels and an aesthetic shopping village nestle among the oak and palmetto woods in this tasteful, get-away-from-it-all idyll. At the northern end of the island lies Fort Clinch State Park, with a 19thC brick fort and a beautiful beach. The island centres on the little town of Fernandina Beach on its western side. Fishing boats moor at the quayside – the shrimping industry began here at the turn of the century. Old brick stores selling flowers, fudge and books line Center St, and you can have a beer and a bowl of shrimps in the Palace Saloon, Florida's oldest. The Chamber of Commerce occupies the decorative old railway depot where Center St meets the docks. But the loveliest part of the town is its residential backstreets, a grid of superb clapboarded Victorian mansions with elaborate verandas and gables. The Amelia Island Museum of History on S 3rd St offers interesting tours of the town.

Apalachicola: 295 miles northwest of Orlando. This is Franklin County – 'Florida's final frontier'. Wrinkled men stand by the roadside in stetsons, while old ladies sell watermelons off the back of trucks. The quiet fishing village of Apalachicola is the county's centre and has a charming Victorian-style hotel. One hundred and fifty years ago, at the height of the cotton industry, it was the third-largest port on the Gulf, distinguished by the many lovely bright-coloured clapboard Victorian houses of wealthy merchants that still line its avenues of oaks dripping with Spanish moss. But today it is known for its seafood: the bay produces 80% of the state's oysters (see **Events**). At the port, piles of shells stand next to tumbledown shacks selling the produce, while heron balance on wooden posts. The village's most famous son is John Gorrie, after whom the small, quirky state museum (0900-1700 Thu.-Mon.; Inexpensive) is named. It contains a reproduction of the ice-making machine that he invented to air-condition rooms, believing malaria could be avoided by lowering the temperature. A long causeway takes you to St. George Island for beautiful white beaches and a state park at the eastern end.

Boca Raton: 45 miles north of Miami. Here, extravagance is the watchword and pink is the colour. This is a resort where stretch limos drop off millionaire swimmers at the beach, and the *haute couture* of wealthy residents and their poodles is on show. It all began in the 1920s when architect Adison Mizner had fanciful plans to create the world's greatest resort. The end of the land boom left him destitute with just The Cloisters, now the luxurious Boca Raton Resort and Club hotel, for posterity (its lavishness is worth just looking at if it's too pricey to experience). 'Boca' honours the architect by painting every-thing possible in the town the same washed pink as the hotel, such as Mizner Park, where any purchase in the avant-garde galleries and fashion boutiques would make a serious dent in your wallet. Parking charges are steep at the three lovely beachside parks.

Busch Gardens: 6 miles northeast of downtown Tampa. Florida's third most popular theme park (after WDW and Sea World) is built round its magnificent collection of over 3300 animals. Don't miss the elephants, the rare white tigers, an excellent bird show and the animal nursery. You can see the park on foot, by rail or by monorail. Try all three for the best views. The terrifying-looking roller coasters give nausea-free rides but be warned before you tackle the water rides that you will get soaked unless you are wearing a plastic coat (on sale in the park). Other entertainment includes a dolphin show, a brewery tour (Budweiser is made here), and various other performances. See TAMPA-ATTRACTIONS.

Clearwater Beach: See Pinellas.

Cypress Gardens: Florida's longest-established tourist park has neither Audio-Animatronics nor roller coasters, but more than makes up for that with natural beauty and a nationally famous water-ski spec-tacular. For the best view of the grounds, hop aboard the Kodak Tower, which slowly rises to a height of 153 ft, and see the botanic garden by boat as early as possible to avoid the queues. The small zoo gardens and the Southern Crossroads Center are both pleasant and relaxed, with good refreshments. See ORLANDO-ATTRACTIONS 3.

Daytona: 53 miles northeast of Orlando. For most tourists Daytona means the world-famous beach and fast cars. The two are even more closely linked, as cars are allowed right onto the hallowed 23 mile-long stretch of white, compacted sands – though there is a 10 mph speed limit! If this, and the predominantly young, strutting beach crowd, don't put you off, then this lively spot is worth a day out, if only to put a face to the famous name. To avoid the invasion of the college crowd, don't go during the last two weeks of Mar. or the first two weeks of April. The only historical attraction is The Casements, former winter home of John D. Rockefeller, at Riverside Drive, Ormond Beach (0900-1700; Free). The Convention and Visitor Bureau is at 126 E Orange Ave, Daytona Beach. For motor-racing fans, the Speed Weeks festival (culminating in the Daytona 500) is held early-mid Feb., and Cycle Week takes place in early Mar. If you'd like a quieter beach resort in the same area, head for New Smyrna, a few miles south.

Epcot: See **Walt Disney World**.

Everglades: This is America's last great subtropical wilderness. Measuring more than half a million hectares, it is home to over 300 species of birds, alligators, snakes, rare crocodiles and the very rare Florida panther. Yet for many tourists the Everglades are a disappointment. There is no dramatic scenery here, and it is not swampland (rather a huge, flat 'sea of grass'). Airboat rides operate only outside the national park boundary. Rides in flimsy-looking insect-like craft touch speeds of up to 60 mph. The experience is both exhilarating and deafening (earplugs are provided). Many airboat centres can be found along Highway 41/Tamiami Trail, and in Everglades City. There are four visitor centres: Gulf Coast, Shark Valley, Main Visitor Center and Flamingo. You can stay in the park at Flamingo or at its edge in Everglades City. However, if you enjoy peace and quiet and appreciate nature (don't expect to see giant, ferocious 'gators, though you will see plenty of small, placid fellows), then the Everglades is a trip you shouldn't miss. Winter is by far the best time to go; not only do birds and animals become more visible as the waters recede and they congregate around remaining sloughs, but the infuriating summer mosquitos are absent.

Note the following Everglades rules: don't feed the wildlife, don't swim anywhere and don't go off on your own. If you do go in summer, cover up well and spray yourself with mosquito repellent. Hurricane Andrew (see **Climate**) devastated the eastern part of the park around the Main Visitor Center but its effects are hardly visible now. See **EVERGLADES-ATTRACTIONS 1 & 2**.

Florida Keys: The Keys are a chain of islands stretching 100 miles southwest from Key Largo through Islamorada, Marathon and the Lower Keys to Key West (see **A-Z**), the southernmost point of the USA. From here Cuba is just 90 miles away. The Keys (the name is derived from the Spanish word *cayo*, meaning 'small island') are often referred to as America's Caribbean islands and they do have a detached, relaxed atmosphere. Apart from those on Key West, there are few man-made attractions. Most activities revolve around the water and specifically around the coral reef, the longest living reef in the western hemisphere. Because of the reef, however, there are few good beaches, the exceptions being at Bahia Honda (Lower Keys) and on Key West. As well as the places outlined (see **FLORIDA KEYS-ATTRACTIONS**), try to see the Faro Blanco Marina, Conch Key and the Natural History Museum of the Keys, all on Marathon. There is a Florida Keys Welcome Center at Key Largo, Highway 1, Mile Marker 106.

Fort Lauderdale: 25 miles north of Miami. Pop: 160,000. Fort Lauderdale is a lively resort with two distinct faces. The 'Strip' beach-front area gained some notoriety from the '60s onwards as the spring-break haunt of raucous college kids. Their legacy partly remains, in the form of some cheap, tacky bars, but this crowd has now mostly moved on to Daytona (see **A-Z**). Behind the long, sandy, well-kept beaches, beautifully landscaped waterways criss-cross their way through the 'Venice of America'. There is nothing cheap about this side of town and a boat trip to see the serried Millionaires' Row is a 'must'. A browse around the Bahia Mar yacht marina is also recommended and some very pleasant waterside dining is based around here. Fort Lauderdale is renowned for its choice of restaurants, boasting some 2500, excluding fast-food joints! By US standards the city is compact and easy to explore. The best way to get started is to take the entertaining and informative 90 min Lolly the Trolley tour ($10, child 7-12 $5). You can get on and off throughout the day. See **FORT LAUDERDALE-ATTRACTIONS**.

Fort Myers: See **Lee Island Coast**.

Jacksonville: 123 miles north of Orlando. This sprawling city cannot compete with Miami, Orlando or Tampa for entertainment or relaxation. Try not to arrive without a proper map. If you're passing through though, it's worth taking a look at Downtown's sleek skyscrap-ers reflecting each other in their glass sides. The broad St. John's River, spanned by impressive bridges, slices the district in two. Head for the waterside Jacksonville Landing shopping and dining complex on the northern side. A water taxi can ferry you across to the boarded Riverwalk, a pleasant escape from the hubbub of the traffic-laden streets. Most of the museums are reachable by car only. The most interesting is the Cummer Gallery of Art (1000-1600 Tue.-Fri., 1200-1700 Sat., 1400-1700 Sun.; Inexpensive), a small, serene place with paintings and a famous collection of early Meissen porcelain. The resort of Jacksonville Beach, 12 miles east, has been offering seaside entertainment and a great beach for over a century. An interesting way

to get to Amelia Island (see **A-Z**) is to travel north up the coast on the
A1A to Mayport. The shacks of the old fishing village vie for attention
with the buzzing helicopters of the large naval base. From here a quaint
car ferry crosses the St. John's River every 30 min.

Jai Alai: Pronounced 'high-a-lie', this is the world's fastest-moving
ball game. It is a version of pelota, which has Spanish Basque origins.
Either eight singles players or eight doubles teams contest each session
of jai alai. The two (or four) players occupy a squash-style court and use
a basket strapped to their wrists to catch and hurl a ball at speeds of up
to 190 mph against any wall except the spectators' fence. As in squash
or tennis, the ball may only bounce once on the floor and a point is
won when the opponent fails to return the ball. A game consists of 7-9
points and there are 12 games per evening session. Play takes place on
a knockout basis, with the better players appearing later on, from games
six or seven, after the less-skilled players have been eliminated.
Although the game is an exciting spectacle in itself, betting is the chief
priority for many spectators and the simplest bet is a $2 (minimum bet)
win. The stadium, or venue, is known as the fronton. See **Sports**.

Key West: 155 miles from Miami. The small Old Town area of Key
West has more shopping, nightlife, restaurants and historic sights than
most places in Florida. Writers and artists such as Ernest Hemingway,
Tennessee Williams and J.J. Audubon have all left their mark on Key
West and helped to establish a bohemian life style and culture. Sloppy
Joe's is still known as Hemingway's bar but it is now much changed.
Duval St is the main shopping street; bars and restaurants cluster
around lively Mallory Square, and everywhere you look are the lovely
terrace and veranda conch (pronounced 'conk') houses – named after
the edible mollusc synonymous with the early Bahamian settlers. Take
the excellent Old Town Trolley Tour to acquaint yourself with Key West
(see **Tours**). You can fly to Key West, but it would be a pity to miss the
scenic drive and other keys en route, and it's better to drive there,
leave your car and fly back to Orlando or Miami. See **FLORIDA KEYS-
ATTRACTIONS**, **Florida Keys**.

Lee Island Coast: Fort Myers is 141 miles northwest of Miami. A profusion of beautiful beaches strewn with shells on the offshore islands slung around Fort Myers attract the cognoscenti to the Lee Island coast. This lovely area has not yet been spoilt by overdevelopment. If you're driving southwards along Highway 141, stop off at the Shell Factory (0900-1800) in North Fort Myers to witness the most phenomenal (and in part tacky) selection of shells on sale that you're ever likely to see. Fort Myers, the region's hub, is nicknamed 'The City of Palms', thanks to the trees that Thomas Edison planted along McGregor Bd. The town's only significant attraction is at 2350 McGregor Bd, where you can visit the Edison-Ford Winter Estates (0900-1600 Mon.-Sat., 1230-1600 Sun.; Expensive). The inventor of the light bulb and much, much more – he owned 1093 patents – Edison created a winter home here in 1886 for health reasons, and in 1915 his friend Henry Ford of automobile fame bought the cottage next door. The laborious 1 hr 40 min tour of their homes and the lovely botanical garden Edison fashioned is worth persisting with for the visit to his reverentially preserved and fusty laboratory. A toll bridge crosses from the mainland to the paradise islands of Sanibel and adjoining Captiva. Exotic birds and plants even surround the supermarket. Luxury resort hotels and choice boutiques lurk among palms, sea grapes and Australian pines, and cycle lanes by the side of the road sum up the pace of life. But the islands' fame rests with their shell beaches (access is limited and parking can be difficult), some of the finest in the world. If you're lucky you might find a conch or sharks' teeth; your best chance is after stormy weather. From Captiva there are shelling and picnic trips to islands only accessible by boat. Along Sanibel's northern coast, you can drive through the J.N. 'Ding' Darling National Wildlife Refuge (dawn-dusk, Sat.-Thu.) and look out for spoonbills, egrets, heron and osprey over the mangrove swamps. For a less exclusive resort, consider Fort Myers Beach, to the south of Fort Myers, whose fine, gently-shelving beach is ideal for kids.

Miami: 232 miles southeast of Orlando. Pop: 1,800,000. Miami is . the largest and most vibrant city in Florida. The actual city of Miami is separated from Miami Beach by its intracoastal waterway and each has

its own identity. The City thrives on its
Downtown business district, known as the
'Wall Street of the South', while the Beach is
devoted to tourism. The Port of Miami is the
world's largest cruise ship terminal and its
airport (see **A-Z**) is the busiest in the southern USA. Around these focal points sprawls a
huge suburban area of 2000 sq miles (see
Orientation). With a Hispanic population of
over 700,000, large parts of Miami are Latin
enclaves – though to the tourist this is only
evident in Little Havana – and sizeable
black, Haitian and Jewish communities add
to the city's cosmopolitan feel. In Downtown
use the Metromover. This is a small driver-
less train which constantly circles a 1.9 mile
loop. At Government Center station
Metromover connects with Metrorail, a
21 mile-long rapid-transit train that runs
north-south between Hialeah and South
Dade. Both systems run 0600-2400. The
following are the main tourist areas:
Art Deco District, Miami Beach: This colour-
ful square mile was built mostly during the
1930s and comprises the world's largest collection of Art Deco architecture. Small hotels
in pastel pink, blue, lavender and green,
neon-lit and streamlined to futuristic shapes,
make up most of the 800 or so Art Deco
buildings in this area. A walk between 6th St
and 23rd St on Ocean Drive will allow you
to see many of the best examples but if you
would like to see more, look along Collins
Ave, Washington Ave and Espanola Way.
The Miami Design Preservation League shop
at the Leslie Hotel, 1244 Ocean Drive is

worth a look, and 90 min walking tours of the area leave from here (1030 Sat.; $6). The tour is not a 'must' but if you are in Miami in Jan. don't miss the Art Deco weekend when everyone dresses up and goes into a wonderful '30s timewarp.

Bayside: This is not a district, but the Marketplace on the bay deserves exploration, whether or not you like shopping. Besides the excellent selection of shops, it features one of Miami's best food courts, nine waterfront restaurants, great views of the 208-berth Miamarina, lots of boat trip possibilities and nonstop live entertainment. HMS *Bounty* – the 1962 MGM film version – is often docked here, and, for a few pieces of silver, you can climb aboard.

Coconut Grove: This beautiful leafy suburb is the oldest part of Miami and retains many reminders of its 19thC development. In many ways it is also the youngest and liveliest district, with its European-style pavement cafés and bars, trendy shops, restaurants and nightspots. Strolling entertainers and impromptu 'street cabaret' are common in the Grove, but if that is not enough there are festivals in mid Jan. (food), mid Feb. (art), early June (Bahamian culture), early Oct. (boat show) and late Dec. (the King Mango Strut Parade!). Explore by day on foot or by bicycle (see **Bicycle Hire**). If you want to visit the Grove on a weekend night, arrive early as it gets very busy.

Coral Gables: The 'City Beautiful' is Miami's most exclusive suburb, developed in the 1920s by George Merrick. Here the sidewalks are painted pink, and it is against the local bylaws to open your garage door for longer than 16 min, lest the area be devalued by the sight of your garage junk! See **MIAMI-EXCURSION**.

Downtown: The best way to view the towering Downtown architecture is to hop on and off the Metromover. Particularly notable are the following giants: the Dade County Courthouse (the grey, pyramid-peaked structure around which turkey vultures constantly hover); the triple-tiered, 47-storey Centrust Tower, brilliantly illuminated at night; the Spanish Baroque Freedom Tower, built in 1925 for the *Miami Daily News* and later used as the Cuban refugee centre (hence its name); and the 55-storey, $200 million Southeast Financial Center, the tallest structure in Miami, complete with a palm tree plaza. The most famous building in Miami, with a palm tree inside its 'hole-in-the-wall', is on Brickell Ave – the Atlantis condominium, which was seen regularly by millions of viewers on the opening shots of *Miami Vice*. *Little Havana:* Miami's Latin Quarter clusters around SW 8th St, or Calle Ocho as it is known locally. The main tourist lure is the proliferation of Spanish/Cuban restaurants but the small shops are also worth a look, particularly if you want some Cuban cigars. If you are in Miami in Mar. don't miss the Carnaval, when a million people take to the streets in one of the world's largest parties. A less boisterous, but still colourful event is the Epiphany festival on 6 Jan.

See **MIAMI**.

Bayside Marketplace

Miami Downtown

Naples: 107 miles northwest of Miami. It's not difficult to see why Naples is apparently the fastest-growing metropolitan area in the US. Manicured lawns, elegant villas and up-market Italianate-style water-front apartments testify to the high quality of life. The town claims more golf courses – 35 at the last count but still increasing – per capita than anywhere else in the world. But you don't need to be a resident or a golf freak to appreciate Naples. A fine wooden fishing pier, constantly rebuilt because of hurricanes, pokes out of a lovely beach backed by trees and gardens. Shoppers can browse in the ritzy fashion boutiques around 3rd St S, where fronts faced with fluted pillars are decked out in pink, salmon and turquoise, or search for souvenirs in the rustic, board-ed Old Marine Marketplace at Tin City. From the harbour alongside, there are a host of fishing and sightseeing boat trips around the Bay of Naples and south to Marco Island. Naples also has some first-rate museums (get a good map or directions as they're awkward to find). The Collier Automotive Museum (1000-1700 Tue.-Sat., 1300-1700 Sun., May-Nov., 1000-1700 Dec.-April; Moderate) has been heralded as the best collection of sports cars in the US. Similarly, the endearing Teddy Bear Museum (1000-1700 Wed.-Sat., 1300-1700 Sun.; Moderate), with some 2300 teddies, is the largest collection for public view in the country. For live animals, Jungle Larry's Zoological Park (0930-1730; Expensive) is worth a visit, but as much for its 52 acres of tropical vegetation of banyans, bamboo and palms as for its caged exhibits. A word of warning: Naples lies on the edge of the subtropical Everglades (see **A-Z**), so watch out for mosquitos in summer. Winter is very much the high season.

Orlando: 232 miles northwest of Miami. Pop: (Greater Orlando) 1,000,000. This busy, prosperous, modern town welcomes over 11 million tourists every year, the vast majority heading straight for Walt Disney World (see **A-Z**) 8 miles away. Its proximity to WDW and its 70,000 hotel beds have firmly established Orlando as a Disney dormi-tory town. But it does have a lot to offer in its own right. Sea World (see **A-Z**) is a truly world-class attraction and Universal Studios Florida (see **A-Z**) is four times the size of the Disney/MGM Theme Park. The neces-sary WDW-linked commercialization of the area has left some of it scarred by treeless highways, chock-a-block with neon-lit fast-food joints, discount stores and tourist traps. Head out a little way, though, and you will discover lakes and greenery in abundance, and nowhere more pleasant than the posh suburb of Winter Park. Downtown Orlando is rapidly developing and next to the excellent Church Street Station a real centre, something lacking in many Florida resorts, is being created. See **ORLANDO**.

Church Street Station

Palm Beach: 70 miles north of Miami. Pop: 250,000. It's worth making the trek to this resort of the super-rich for two reasons: the Henry Morrison Flagler Museum, known as Whitehall, and Worth Ave. Henry Morrison Flagler (1830-1913), a founder of the Standard Oil Co. with John D. Rockefeller, was the man who brought the railroad to southern

Florida, thereby establishing Palm Beach and Miami, among other resorts. Whitehall is more a stately home than a museum and its great halls, music room, billiards room, library, dining rooms and bedrooms, mostly decorated in historic European styles, are fit for kings and queens (1000-1700 Tue.-Sat., 1200-1700 Sun.; Moderate). Worth Ave is recognized as one of the world's great shopping streets, with over 250 stores. Such names as Cartier, Gucci and Saks 5th Avenue are taken for granted here. But it is not just the famous names that make Worth Ave great; it is the atmosphere conjured up by the manicured palms and beautiful Spanish architecture. If you can tear yourself away, the best beaches are at Jupiter, a few miles north, and Lake Worth, which has most water-sport facilities, a mile or two south.

Panama City Beach: 334 miles northwest of Orlando. Neon, motels, crazy golf, go-karting, fast-food stalls, Daiquiri Expresses, nightclubs – such is the heady concoction of this massive cheep 'n' cheerful resort. It's busiest in the spring break in Mar. and early April when up to 150,000 students descend; in summer it attracts all types. The superb beach is some 27 miles long, but in season don't expect to have any of it to yourself. Every type of water sport is available (see **Water Sports**). The heart of the resort contains the Miracle Strip Amusement Park, an old-fashioned funfair with a roller coaster and a big wheel, and next door Shipwreck Island Water Park. There's also a marine park and zoo. For a more sedate time head east to the dune-backed beaches of the St. Andrews State Park, from where you can take a ferry shuttle to Shell Island for beachcombing. Nearby, from Treasure Island Marina you can try out every type of boating activity, from deep-sea fishing to snorkelling and sailing.

Pensacola: 428 miles northwest of Orlando. Were it not for a hurricane that disrupted the Spanish settlers who came in 1559, Pensacola, not St. Augustine (see **A-Z**), would be the country's oldest city. Nonetheless, Pensacola has an interesting historical heritage. At the foot of the 3 mile bridge that takes you across Pensacola Bay into the city lies the visitor centre, where you can pick up a particularly good historical guide. Of the city's three understated historical districts, Seville, established in 1752 by Spanish colonists, is the most rewarding, focused around a lovely square with gazebos, oaks, magnolia and old-fashioned street lamps. Within the Seville district lies Historic Pensacola Village (1000-1600 Mon.-Sat.; Moderate), a collection of museums and old buildings round Zaragoza St, and the Pensacola Historical Museum (0900-1630 Mon.-Sat.; Inexpensive) in an old red-brick church. Head up Palafox, the pleasantly restored downtown centre with brick pavements, to North Hill, a 50-block area of detached cottages and opulent mansions built between the 1870s and the 1930s in a multitude of styles. But if you visit just one sight, follow the signs out of the city southwest to the National Museum of Naval

Aviation (0900-1700; Free), within the Pensacola Naval Air Station compound. Its vast collection of planes, from biplanes to modern jets, is superbly displayed. Make sure you see the fighters salvaged from the sea and left in their barnacled state, and the full-size replica of part of an aircraft carrier. 'The whitest beaches in the world' claim the billboards for the barrier islands to the south of the city, part of the 150 mile-long Gulf Islands National Seashore. Here you can seek out sands backed by unspoilt dunes, or a busy daytime and night-time scene at Pensacola Beach Resort on Santa Rosa Island.

Pinellas, The: The overpopulated thumb of land between Tampa Bay and the Gulf of Mexico largely consists of a vast residential grid. Apart from visits to St. Petersburg (see **A-Z**), tourists stick to the 25 miles of barrier islands along the west coast. A virtually continuous drag of resort development, PR talk calls it 'The Suncoast' for its high sunshine quota. On one side are spacious beaches with fine sand and plenty of water sports (see **A-Z**); on the other a channel of water where marinas offer fishing and sightseeing cruises. In between, the resorts themselves feel cramped and traffic-laden. Clearwater Beach is a trendy young person's place, famous for its volleyball tournaments. Treasure Island has the widest beach on the stretch, its sand intermingled with crushed shells. At the southern end, pleasant Pass-A-Grille is more of a local community, less of a resort. The oddest local sight is the Boatyard Village (1000-1900 Mon.-Thu., 1000-2100 Fri. & Sat., 1200-1800 Sun.), hidden away beside Tampa Bay and close to St. Petersburg/Clearwater Airport – a New England-style fishing village of ageing wood and tin turned into an arts and crafts shopping emporium. There's a similar boardwalk shopping arrangement at John's Pass Village at Madeira Beach. At Indian Shores, there's a seabird sanctuary to visit: many pelicans, cumbersome birds so vast that they momentarily blot out the sun as they pass overhead, inhabit the area. See **Tarpon Springs**.

Pleasure Island: See **Walt Disney World**.

St. Augustine: 98 miles north of Orlando. Founded in 1565, this city is quite simply the oldest in the US. Wherever you go, signs tell you that you're looking at the oldest this or the oldest that. Within the historic district lies a multitude of sites which make up a good day's sightseeing. Trolley and horse and carriage tours leave from near the visitor centre at 10 Castillo Drive. But as St. Augustine is quaint and sleepy, pick up a map from the centre and explore on foot. For highlights, make for the waterfront to visit the imposing 17thC Castillo de San Marcos made from coquina, a hard rock of compacted shells and coral. Take pedestrianized St. George St past wooden-shuttered houses that contain arts and crafts shops, leafy bars and cafés, and hide shaded courtyards behind. On the way visit the Oldest Wooden Schoolhouse and the restored Spanish Quarter, where eight homes re-create, with the help of performing costumed actors, Spanish colonial life in the 1740s. At the far end of the old district, among lovely wooden villas and cobbled backstreets, stands the fascinating Oldest House, with a 400 year history and adapted successively by the Spanish, British and Americans. Towers and arches make Flagler College the city's most striking building, built in 1885 by the oil millionaire Henry Flagler as the Ponce de Leon Hotel in an early attempt to draw tourists to Florida. Across the square, what was once the Alcazar Hotel now houses the Lightner Museum, best known for its first-rate collection of Tiffany and cut glass. A couple of miles east lie Anastasia State Park and the impressive St. Augustine Beach.

St. Petersburg: 105 miles southwest of Orlando. The glue that holds the Pinellas (see **A-Z**) together, affluent and spacious St. Petersburg – or 'St. Pete' to the locals – seems awash with trees and grassy parks. Promoted since the turn of the century as a resort for its healthy climate, for a long time it had the reputation of 'Retirement City', but the average age of the population is rapidly dropping. A garish modern pier in pink and turquoise provides its focal point; it ends in an upside-down pyramid of cafés, restaurants, boutiques and a small aquarium, while outside pelicans swoop over cruise boats. For culture vultures, the wide-ranging Museum of Fine Arts (1000-1700 Tue.-Sat., 1300-1700 Sun.; Donation), in a pillared villa near the base of the pier, ably represents the French Impressionists and has finely furnished rooms of different periods. More exceptional, and justifying a visit to the city in its own right, the Dali Museum (0930-1730 Tue.-Sat., 1200-1730 Sun. & Mon.; Moderate) holds nothing less than the world's largest collection – over 1000 works of art – by the surrealist artist, chronologically displayed. You might consider leaving the kids in Great Explorations (1000-1700 Mon.-Sat., 1200-1700 Sun.; Inexpensive), just a block away from the Dali Museum, a hands-on science playground primarily for young children. At the other end of town, the Sunken Gardens (0900-1700; Moderate), a more sedate and somewhat overpriced experience, have lovely tropical gardens inhabited by parrots and other exotic birds.

Sarasota: 127 miles southwest of Orlando. It's hard not to be bowled over by the smart coastal town of Sarasota. Fascinating museums, top performing arts, up-market shopping, great beaches – this is one of Florida's most appealing destinations. Number one on the list of attractions are the unmissable Ringling Museums (1000-1730, until 2200 Thu., Oct.-June; Moderate). On the northern edge of town, the complex houses a major collection of medieval, Renaissance and 17thC European art put together by multimillionaire and owner

of the Ringling Brothers Circus, John Ringling, in the 1920s and '30s. In the dazzlingly beautiful courtyard abutting the gallery, reproductions of the world's most famous statues peer at you from all angles. The circus had its winter headquarters here from 1927 to 1960, and a further museum houses circus paraphernalia such as wagons, exotic costumes and a silver cannon. At the seaside edge of the estate, the Ringling winter home, Ca'd'Zan (Venetian for 'The House of John') is nothing less than a showy palace covered in multicoloured tiles. The elaborate rooms each plagiarize a formal style of architecture. Opposite the Ringling complex, in its own way Bellm's Cars and Music of Yesterday (0830-1800 Mon.-Sat., 0930-1800 Sun.; Moderate) is equally absorbing, a mindboggling array of musical boxes in a vast warehouse, and a first-rate display of pristine automobiles, from BMW bubble cars to Cadillacs and sports cars. For your last sightseeing port of call, head downtown to Selby Gardens (1000-1700; Moderate), where you can learn everything you wanted to know about the state's flora and study orchids and banyans in a beautiful waterside setting. But many are lured to Sarasota for its sophisticated air. As one of Florida's main cultural centres it has its own ballet, orchestra and opera, and a top theatre company (phone the 24 hr artsline on 813-359-ARTS for details of what's on). For shopping and dining there are the chic galleries and antique shops of Palm Ave, the trendy ethnic restaurants of Sarasota Quay that stands by elegant marinas and waterside condominiums, and, on its own barrier island, St. Armand's Circle, a giant mall around an overblown roundabout. Most tourists base themselves at Lido, exclusive Longboat and Siesta Keys, all with excellent beaches.

Sea World: This is the world's most popular marine-life park. Sea World is a wholesome mix of fun, education and marine research. The best shows are at the Sea Lion and Otter Stadium, the Whale and Dolphin Stadium, and the Shamu Stadium (Shamu is a 6000 lb killer whale). The Terrors of the Deep and Penguin Encounter are both 'musts' and the tropical reef is recommended. The park's newest residents are Florida's own ugly and remarkably tame manatees. After dark Shamu and family's Night Magic is a great spectacle, and there are fireworks and laser shows. Allow a full day for a visit. See **ORLANDO-ATTRACTIONS 1**.

Sea World

Spaceport USA (NASA Kennedy Space Center): 45 miles east of Orlando. If you are remotely interested in space exploration, then Spaceport USA is, as it claims, Florida's best value for visitors. Within the large, free visitor area there are cinema films, a towering display of historic space rockets, the Animatronic-hosted Satellites and You exhibit, and various other show areas to see. Don't miss *The Dream is Alive* film which shows the thunderous launch of the Space Shuttle and daily life in outer space. Shot on special IMAX film by the astronauts themselves, and projected onto a five-storey-high screen, you'll think you too are aboard. New to the centre is a full-scale model of a proposed space station. Opt for the red bus tour to see the shuttle; the blue tour goes to Cape Canaverel where the emphasis is on the early space programme. The tour is interesting but on the long side (2 hr), and for security reasons you never get very close to the Shuttle. Buy your tickets for the film and the bus tour as early as possible to avoid queueing. Allow a total of 5-6 hr for your visit. See **ORLANDO-ATTRACTIONS 3.**

Tallahassee: 242 miles northwest of Orlando. Tallahassee was chosen as state capital in 1824, being midway between the earlier regional capitals of St. Augustine and Pensacola. It seems an unlikely centre
of government now, its tree-canopied streets and 19thC mansions giv-
ing it a Deep South flavour far removed from the brashness of southern
Florida. The visitor centre in the foyer of the stark concrete tower block
of the New Capitol has walking tour details around the prettiest residential streets, or you can hop on the free trolley bus. Behind the New
Capitol, the Old Capitol (0900-1630 Mon.-Fri., 1000-1630 Sat., 1200-
1630 Sun.; Free) has been restored to its turn-of-the-century state, with
elegant chambers inside and a façade of chunky pillars and red and
white striped awnings. A short stroll west from the New Capitol, the
imaginative Museum of Florida History (see Old Capitol for times;
Free) offers everything from the bones of a mastodon to displays on
citrus fruit-farming. Wakulla Springs State Park lies 15 miles south on
the SR61, and is where *Tarzan* movies were made in the 1930s. You
can take a glass-bottomed boat on the pool above one of the world's
deepest springs and a river boat trip for jungle wildlife spotting.

Tampa: 85 miles west of Orlando. If you're looking for beaches, skip
Tampa and head on west to the Pinellas (see **A-Z**). Stop for a day or
two if you're interested in experiencing a buzzing city that's on the up,
with plenty of sport and culture to grab your interest. As in most
American cities, a car is vital to get around the urban sprawl: the main
attractions such as Busch Gardens (see **A-Z**) and Adventure Island lie
in the northern suburbs, a 20 min drive from the city centre.
Downtown, bulldozers are eradicating any trace of the old to make
way for the growing crop of modern skyscrapers that act as a useful
orientation point. The Museum of Art and the Henry Flagler Museum
are within walking distance of the visitor centre at 111 Madison St. A
monorail goes from Downtown to Harbor Island, a big shopping and
entertainment complex vibrant at night with live music and moonlit
pedalo rides. But Tampa's most rewarding area to explore is Ybor City,
founded in 1886 and once the biggest cigar-producing centre in the
world. After a troublesome century of commercial decline and urban
renewal, this Cuban neighbourhood has been revivified as a bohemian

landmark district. An old cigar factory has been converted into Ybor Square, a trendy shopping mall. Within the old brick buildings with wrought-iron balconies along 7th Ave, you can still buy hand-rolled cigars or hang out in Cuban cafés. Many of the shops have been converted into art galleries, and at night it seems that every young person in Tampa comes here for the raucous and varied music scene of everything from jazz and blues to heavy rock. At 2117 E 7th Ave you can find the original, multitiled Columbia Restaurant, the oldest Spanish restaurant in the US.

Tarpon Springs: 100 miles west of Orlando. It seems fanciful to imagine a Greek island harbour off the coast of Florida, but this is exactly how Tarpon Springs appears. A Greek community settled here in 1905 to dive for sponges. Decline in the 1940s followed prosperity, after disease affected the sponge beds. Now the decks of boats moored in the harbour may equally be piled with sponges and shrimp. Sponges of every size – some for the car, some for the bath – ooze from shopfronts in stores such as the Athens Gift Shop. You can snack on baklava in the Hellas Bakery or dine on taramasalata and dolmas in a choice of Greek restaurants. Spongeorama (1000-1700) introduces you to the community's history, and sponge catching and processing. See **Pinellas**.

Treasure Island: See **Pinellas**.

Universal Studios Florida: This is the third most popular theme park in the US. There's much more to see here than at Disney/MGM Studios. Visitors are promised the most spectacular and technically advanced entertainment of its kind through the use of themed rides and live interactive shows. For thrills and chills, take a cable-car ride to be threatened by a 30 ft-high, banana-breathed King Kong, experience an earthquake that's 8.3 on the Richter scale, or board a boat to come nose-to-snout with the 32 ft, 3 tonne killer shark from *Jaws*. For emotion of a very different kind, hop aboard a star-bound bicycle to help E.T. save his ailing planet. If you want to know more about horror and suspense, go to Alfred Hitchcock: The Art of Making Movies or The Gory, Gruesome and Grotesque Horror Make-Up Show. Kids will love the simulation of getting into a Hanna-Barbera high-speed chase cartoon and seeing such favourites as The Flintstones, Yogi Bear, Huckleberry Hound and Scooby Doo. There are over 40 restaurants,

including Mel's Drive-in from *American Graffiti* on Hollywood Bd, while other street set locations include San Francisco Wharf, a New England village and even New York City! See **ORLANDO-ATTRACTIONS 1**.

Walt Disney World (WDW): This is the world's number one holiday attraction, recording over 25 million paid visits per year. It occupies a huge, 43 square mile site and comprises three major theme parks (Magic Kingdom, Epcot, Disney/MGM Studios), two water parks (River Country, Typhoon Lagoon), a zoological park (Discovery Island), an evening entertainment complex (Pleasure Island), a shopping 'village' (Disney Village), a campground with numerous outdoor facilities (Fort Wilderness) and 21 hotel resorts, each one of them open to the public. The Magic Kingdom is the 'spiritual centre' of WDW, the place every child (of every age) wants to visit; 'grown-ups' will probably get a bigger kick out of Epcot or Disney/MGM Studios, but it would be a shame to miss any part of this amazing world. Among the armoury of special effects that Disney employs throughout the parks are Animatronics and Circlevision. The former are lifelike wax-model robots (of people and animals) which move, and often talk or make sounds (Audio-Animatronics). Circlevision is a system of film projection in which a number of projectors and screens are used to surround the viewer totally. The effect is to make you think that you are actually in the middle of the scene (akin to a simulator) and is particularly effective with huge panoramic shots. To all intents and purposes you are actually flying (or travelling by boat, train, etc.) through Canada, France, China, or wherever is being shown on screen. You can see to both sides, ahead (where you are going) and behind (where you have just been). The least-crowded times to visit are Jan. through to the 1st week in Feb., Sep. through to Nov.

Epcot, Walt Disney World

(except Thanksgiving weekend), and from Thanksgiving to the beginning of the Christmas holidays. The peak periods are mid June-mid Aug. and all holiday times, particularly Christmas. Although there is a special magic to WDW at Christmas, it is not worth making your first trip there at this time, nor at any other peak period, unless you enjoy queueing all day and night. However, even at the quietest time 45-60 min queues form. To beat these, arrive at the entrance when the park opens (all open 30 min before the official time, i.e. usually 0830), head straight for the farthest point and start off on the most popular attractions, then work your way back to the entrance. The busiest days are Mon.-Wed. at Magic Kingdom and Epcot, and Wed.-Fri. at Disney/MGM. You will need at least four days to see the three parks, so if you can afford it a four-day passport to all three parks will show savings on the daily rate (one-day ticket $34, child 3-9 $27; four-day pass $125, child $98; five-day pass $170, child $135).

Magic Kingdom: As the Cinderella Castle looms ahead and the strains of *When You Wish Upon a Star* hit you, you'll realize why this is called the Magic Kingdom. There are six themed areas, or lands, boasting over 40 attractions, most of them rides. It is impossible for you to do them all in a day – the queues won't let you. You'll need one and a half to two full days to see everything here. In addition to the rides selected in **WDW-MAGIC KINGDOM**, younger children will enjoy most of Mickey's Birthdayland and Fantasyland, and in Frontierland, the Country Bear Jamboree and Tom Sawyer's Island. You can easily walk around the park but riding on the WDW Railroad, and particularly the Skyway, are highly recommended. Daily events include a carnival procession and (when park hours are extended) SpectroMagic, a spectacular laser show with Disney characters, plus Fantasy in the Sky, a pyrotechnics extravaganza.

Epcot: Walt Disney's Experimental Prototype Community of Tomorrow (EPCOT) was first conceived in 1966 and its Future World section (see **WDW-EPCOT FUTURE WORLD**) still retains Walt's original objective of 'showing off the latest US technologies and the imagination of free enterprise'. This is most clearly shown in such pavilions as the World of Motion but tends to get a little lost when more abstract subjects, such as Imagination, are tackled. Here the emphasis is less on thrill rides and more on education, by the use of films and some excellent hands-on experimental areas. It's all great fun but sometimes you have to work hard to make it really mind-expanding. The other half of Epcot is World Showcase (see **WDW-EPCOT WORLD SHOWCASE**), where 11 countries have done an often remarkable job of turning a few square yards of Florida into Morocco, Japan, Mexico and so on. Each national pavilion has its own architectural centrepiece, shops and at least one restaurant (see **ORLANDO-RESTAURANTS**). Most feature either a ride or a Circlevision film. The best entertainment is often provided by national street performers, ranging from folk dancers and comedy players to bagpipers and Oriental drums. The food here is excellent and alcohol is served. Don't miss Illuminations, the grand finale every evening. It will probably be the best lights, laser and fireworks spectacular you have ever seen! Allow at least two days to see the whole of Epcot.

Disney/MGM Studios: This is the most adult-orientated of the three

parks. The theme tune from *Gone with the Wind* replaces *When You Wish Upon a Star*, Harrison Ford takes the place of Peter Pan, and for the Wicked Queen read *Alien*! Nostalgia is a key element and on Hollywood Boulevard you are transported back to the '30s and '40s. There are few Animatronics figures here and only one thrill ride (Star Tours), though it is one of the best in WDW. However, the live action of the Indiana Jones set and the opportunity to meet one of the Teenage Mutant Ninja Turtles will keep most kids happy, and adults will be intrigued to see behind the scenes. The 3-D Muppet Show astonishes young and old alike, as does the superb animation in *The Voyage of the Little Mermaid*. Make sure to be around at 1100 or 1530 for the fun of Aladdin's Royal Caravan Procession. Allow one full day to visit the studios. See **WDW-DISNEY/MGM THEME PARK**.

Pleasure Island: This night-time entertainment complex for adults features all the high technology and special effects you would expect from Disney. A single payment of $13.95 allows you entry to all the clubs on the island. These include Mannequins (a high-energy, state-of-the-art disco featuring Animatronics, dancing mannequins and a revolving dance floor), Neon Armadillo (a live country music saloon), Comedy Warehouse (a comedy club which does a hilarious extended sketch on the joys of being a tourist in 'Wallet Disney World') and the Adventurers Club (a 1930s traveller's club where Animatronics embellish amusing and outrageous tales). There are also shops, street players and a choice of restaurants. Eat early and aim to do three clubs in a night, and don't miss the nightly 'New Year's Eve' 2300 or 2400 firework celebrations. See **ORLANDO-NIGHTLIFE**.

For details of Fort Wilderness, Discovery Island, River Country and Typhoon Lagoon, see **WDW-OTHER ATTRACTIONS**. For Disney Village Marketplace, see **ORLANDO-SHOPPING**.

Weeki Wachee Spring: 78 miles west of Orlando. 0930-1730; Expensive. Mermaids perform Hans Christian Andersen's *The Little Mermaid* underwater. There are also jungle river cruises, bird shows and a children's zoo. Buccaneer Bay spring-water park (0900-1700 April-Aug.; Moderate) is just next door.

Naples

ACC

Accidents & Breakdowns: In the event of an accident, exchange names, addresses and insurance details. To contact the emergency services, tel: 911. If someone is injured or you are held responsible, insist on contacting your embassy or consulate (see **A-Z**). All traffic accidents must be reported to the local police or Highway Patrol (see **Police**). In the case of a breakdown ring the number your car hire firm gave you. If you break down on a highway, lift up the bonnet of your car and wait in the vehicle for assistance from Highway Patrol. Don't open your doors or windows to anyone else. See **Driving**.

Accommodation: The standard of hotel accommodation in Florida is high, with colour TV, two large double beds and air-conditioning the norm in all rooms. Many hotels also boast a swimming pool. Prices usually quoted are per room, excluding breakfast. The term 'hotel resort' refers to a large, usually luxury complex with all tourist facilities on site. Efficiencies and pullmanettes are simple bed-sitting rooms with cooking facilities. If you are touring on a budget, you may spend most nights in comfortable but unimaginative chain hotels/motels. Most are located on the commercial outskirts of cities or by the beach in Gulf coast resorts. Reckon on paying $50 per night per double room. Orlando has a huge choice of accommodation to suit all pockets. Off-season competition is fierce and you will find good-quality rooms available from as little as $35 per night. Many Orlando hotels will offer a 'children stay free' deal, or charge a nominal amount. Before you go, write to the Orlando tourist office for the official visitor's guide, which includes many special accommodation discount offers (see **Tourist Information**). Hotels in Miami are similarly well-appointed, though considerably more expensive. WDW offers some splendid hotels. The Caribbean Beach Resort is the cheapest (from $89); most others offer rooms from $180. The only obvious advantage to staying at WDW is convenience – you will still have to queue for rides and you will get few discount privileges. To arrange accommodation in WDW, contact WDW Central Reservation Office, Box 10100, Lake Buena Vista, FL 32830-0100, tel: 407-WDISNEY.

During the peak winter season, nominally 15 Dec.-Easter (although late Jan.-early Feb. is quiet), it is advisable to prebook all accommodation. If you arrive in Orlando without a reservation, go to the Visitor Information Center on International Drive. In Miami, tel: 305-5382540 for reservations. If you plan on staying in the Florida Keys outside of Key West, tel: 305-4511414 (Keys Welcome Center) or if you want to stay in Key West, tel: 305-2964444 (Key West Welcome Center). General price ranges for accommodation per room are as follows:

	Orlando	Miami	Key West
Luxury	over $90	over $100	over $150
Moderate	$60	$80	$90
Budget	$40	$40	$60

In addition there is a 6% State sales tax. In Miami as much as an extra 6.5% local tax may be levied on your hotel bill. A room with an ocean view will be considerably more expensive than its equivalent with, say, a pool or garden view. See **Camping & Caravanning**, **Youth Hostels**.

Airports: Direct flights from the UK operate to Miami and Orlando only. Orlando Airport is 11 miles from International Drive ($30 by taxi, including tip) and 14 miles from WDW ($14 by regular shuttle bus, $40 by taxi, including tip). Miami International Airport (MIA) is 8 miles from Downtown ($15 by taxi, including tip) and 14 miles from South Miami Beach ($22 by taxi, including tip). MIA is one of the largest and busiest airports in the world and has every facility. All car hire firms are based in or near the airports. Note that there are no luggage (baggage) trolleys available and the choice is either to carry, or to hire a porter (see **Tipping**). Distances in Florida are large. Consider flying long distances within the state. US Air offers two-, three- or four-coupon air passes ($179, $229 and $279 respectively). Tickets must be booked before departure from the UK, tel: 0800-777333. Details of your first flight must be fixed, as must the route for your subsequent flights.

Baby-sitters: Many resort hotels provide a baby-sitting service and all hotels should be able to provide a list of State-approved sitters. At WDW, both the Magic Kingdom and Epcot have excellent Baby-Care Centers. See **Children**.

Banks: See **Currency**, **Money**, **Opening Times**.

Beaches: The only place you're likely to visit in Florida where you won't be near a beach is Orlando. Both Gulf and Atlantic coast beaches are spectacularly beautiful. Both have busy, trendy spots (Daytona and Miami Beach in the east, Clearwater and the Pinellas beaches in the west), where you'll find every water sport imaginable (see **Water Sports**), volleyball courts, and a

family atmosphere or a lively young crowd depending on the time of year. Elsewhere are more exclusive, peaceful haunts – the famous shell beaches of Sanibel and Captiva, and numerous state parks with board-walks over dunes, and well-kept facilities. Most popular beaches have lifeguards. The waters of the Gulf are warmer but murkier than those of the Atlantic. The keys have few good beaches, the main exceptions being on Key West. See MIAMI-BEACHES.

Best Buys: Orlando caters for a family market and the shops on and around International Drive offer discounts on just about everything to do with the home and clothing. You will also find discounts on a lot of Disney merchandise, but the quality is often poor and you would be as well buying Mickey and Goofy souvenirs from WDW. At Epcot you can buy souvenirs from China, Japan and nine other countries, but don't expect the prices to be Far East. Miami shopping is stylish and trendy, and everywhere you look there are great T-shirts. Local specialities include Indian crafts at the Miccosukee Indian Village (see EVERGLADES-ATTRACTIONS 1), Cuban cigars in Little Havana (see **Miami**), and citrus fruit (although you will get exactly the same at home cheaper). In the smartest resorts, such as Naples or Boca Raton, prices in the malls are sky-high. In unpretentious resorts such as Panama City Beach or Clearwater, you can pick up five T-shirts for $10. Many museum shops carry excellent goods. See MIAMI-SHOPPING, ORLANDO-SHOPPING, **Markets**, **Shopping**.

Bicycle & Motorcycle Hire: Many resorts offer bicycle hire. It is highly recommended in the scenic Miami suburbs of Coconut Grove and Coral Gables (see MIAMI-EXCURSION). Both have special cycle paths. Get hold of the excellent *Bicycle Street Map* published by the Metro-Dade Bicycle-Pedestrian Department, tel: 305-3754507. Bikes for hire are available from Dade Cycles, 3216 Grand Ave, Coconut Grove (0930-1730 Mon.-Fri., 1030-1730 Sun.). Elsewhere, parts of the Everglades are perfect for cycling and bikes are for hire at Shark Valley and Flamingo. Orlando itself is not so suited to cycling, but Fort Wilderness at WDW is another good cycling location. Motorcycle hire is rare in Florida, as four wheels are generally considered safer than two.

Budget: 1993 prices.

Accommodation	See **A-Z**
Breakfast	$2-3 light meal; $4-6 full buffet
Lunch	$5 burger and drink
Dinner	From $15
Tea/coffee/soft drink	75c-$1.25
Beer	$1 draught; $2-3 bottle
Discos/nightclubs	$3-10
Museums	$1-10
Theme parks	$15-35
WDW	$34; child $27; car parking $5 (one-day ticket)

Note that many establishments display prices exclusive of the 6% State sales tax. Tipping (see **A-Z**) will also add a hefty chunk to your bill. Children get reductions at most attractions and senior citizens will also usually get a discount (though they may have to ask for one). Money-off and special-deal coupons are common for accommodation, restaurants and virtually every attraction except WDW (everything – food, drink, T-shirts – costs more in the theme parks). These can be picked up, free, in your hotel lobby and at tourist offices and visitor centres (see **Tourist Information**). Restaurants are particularly promotion-conscious, with all-you-can-eat, 2 for 1 and happy hours almost everywhere.

Buses: The only places you might consider using buses are Miami and Orlando, and here they are designed for local use and are of limited help in getting to and from tourist destinations. The service in Orlando (75c per ride) is almost nonexistent in the evenings if you're staying at WDW. In Miami all fares are $1.25 (exact change), regardless of distance. Leaflets are available at the Government Center Metrorail station detailing links with Metrorail (see **Miami**).

Cameras & Photography: Buy your films from a supermarket or drugstore to get the best price (around $4 for a 24-exposure, 35 mm film). Even if you don't own a camera, many theme parks will lend you one for the day and just charge you for the film. As heat can affect the quality of film, keep your spare films in a fridge if possible and never leave them in a car in the sun.

Camping & Caravanning: There are over 700 camp sites in Florida covering all the resort areas. These cater for both tents and camper vans (Recreational Vehicles or RVs). All have a laundry and 'full hook-up' (mains connections), and the majority have a swimming pool and recreational facilities. Prices average around $30 per night. Fort Wilderness at WDW charges around $50 per night for full hook-up sites. For the *Florida Camping Directory*, contact Florida Campground Association, 1638 N Plaza Drive, Tallahassee, FL 32308-5364, tel: 904-6568878. Note that camping on the roadside, in a car park or on any private land without the owner's permission is not only illegal but unsafe.

Car Hire: In order to see anything of Florida you have to hire a car. You must be 21 and possess a full UK licence or an International Driving Permit. It's much cheaper to arrange car hire in advance from the UK. Expect to pay around £70 per week for hire and Collision Damage Waiver (CDW). Beware that the prices quoted for car hire in Florida – as low as $65 per week unlimited mileage – do not include anything other than basic third-party insurance. In the land of multimillion-dollar litigation suits, and where many drivers are underinsured or totally uninsured, you need at least the following: CDW – without this you could be liable for the cost of any damage to your vehicle, however it has been caused, or even the full cost if it is stolen (typical cost $11 per day); Personal Liability Insurance/Extended Protection – this increases the cover of claims against you from the inadequate mandatory cover of $100,000 to a more realistic $1 million (typical cost $2.50 per day). There are additional insurance covers for personal injury/death, theft of luggage, etc. When budgeting, remember to add the State tax (6%), car hire tax ($2.05 per day) and in some cases a further airport tax of up to 10%. The daily rate is relatively much more expensive than the weekly rate. The standard of hire cars (usually automatic) is very good, with air-conditioning and a stereo radio as standard fittings. See **Crime & Theft**, **Driving**.

Chemists: Nonprescription medicines are available from any chemist (drugstore/pharmacy), normally open 0900-2100/2200 Mon.-Sat. In Orlando, 24 hr drugstores are: Eckerd Drugs, 908 Lee Rd, tel: 407-6446908; and Walgreen Drugstore, 2410 E Colonial Drive, tel: 4907-8946781. In Miami, 24 hr drugstores are: Eckerd Drugs, 1825 NE Miami Gardens Drive, 185th St, North Miami Beach, tel: 305-9325740; and 9031 SW 107th Ave, tel: 305-2746776. Some chemists will deliver locally. See **Health**.

Children: In terms of weather and entertainment central Florida is a children's paradise. It doesn't come cheap, however: a day at WDW and a day at Busch Gardens, two 'musts', will cost two adults and two children over nine years old more than $270 just in admission fees and car parking. Kids may also take a dislike to queueing hour upon hour at WDW, so avoid the peak periods. See **Baby-sitters**.

Climate: Summer (June-Sep.) temperatures in Miami rarely fall below an afternoon average of 30°C. You will need a light sweater or jacket while you are indoors, however, due to the air-conditioning. Winter is more variable, with an average afternoon temperature of 24-27°C, but during Dec. and Jan. temperatures may drop to near-freezing for a short period. June-Nov. is the wet (and hurricane) season. Humidity is high (often uncomfortably so), storms frequent and sunshine unreliable. As a general rule, the Keys are 3-4°C warmer than Miami all year round, while Orlando is cooler in the winter (by up to 6° C). The most comfortable times to go to Florida are Oct.-Nov. and April-May.

One of America's worst natural disasters struck Florida on 24 August 1992. Hurricane Andrew, with winds of up to 200 mph, was the strongest hurricane to hit Florida in 50 years. The eye of the storm swept in a strip across southern Florida through South Miami and the top of the Everglades. However, the only two attractions to have closed indefinitely are the Weeks Air Museum and the Gold Coast Railroad Museum, both in Miami.

Complaints: If you have been overcharged, or find that prices do not correspond with those displayed, ask to see the owner or manager of the premises (note that it is not the practice in the US to include taxes in prices displayed). If you are still not satisfied, then you can report the establishment to the police or contact the Consumer Service Office in the Department of Agriculture, tel: 904-4882221. Just threatening this course of action may prove sufficient.

Consulates: The only British consulate in Florida is in Miami, at Suite 2110, Brickell Bay Office Tower, 1001 S Bayshore Drive, tel: 305-3741522.

Conversion Chart:

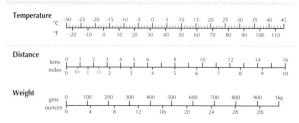

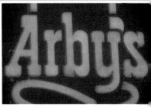

Credit Cards: See **Money**.

Crime & Theft. There has recently been a number of attacks on tourists
in Florida. Most of the incidents have occurred in Miami, with a few in
Orlando. However, you should not drop your guard anywhere in the state,
even in the much safer-feeling Gulf coast resorts. While statistically it is
very unlikely that you will face any danger, take the following precautions.
If you arrive at Miami Airport at night, take a taxi to your hotel and pick up
your hire car the following day. Make sure that you have good road and
city maps (particularly for Miami and Orlando). Study your route carefully
before setting off: it is all too easy to miss a turning off a main road and
end up in an insalubrious area, such as Liberty Town and Overtown in
Miami. Ask at the car hire office or your hotel for the names of 'no-go'
neighbourhoods. In Miami, more 'tourist-friendly' signposts to attractions
and the airport have been put up to help tourists find their way around.
Thieves and muggers were once able to identify hire cars by the initial 'Y'
or 'Z' on the numberplate. Replacement numberplates do not have these:
make sure this is the case with your hire car. If you are lost do not stop to
ask for directions or to study your map; instead, drive to the nearest well-lit
public place. Likewise, if your car is being bumped from behind, if you see
someone on the road who needs help, or if a passing motorist says something is wrong with your vehicle, do not stop but drive to the nearest public place and seek assistance, or call the police (see **A-Z**) on 911. In downtown areas use valet parking offered by hotels and clubs rather than parking the car yourself (see **Parking**). Remember also to lock your car and
hotel room at all times, to leave large amounts of cash in the hotel's safe-
deposit facility, and not to flaunt any jewellery while walking in the street.
Hotels, car hire companies and tourist bureaux are very security conscious
and can provide plenty of helpful advice. For up-to-date information, contact the Foreign Office's Travel Advice Unit, tel: 071-2704129.
See **Consulates**, **Insurance**.

Currency: The dollar ($) is the US monetary unit, divided into 100 cents (c).
Coins – 1c (penny), 5c (nickel), 10c (dime), 25c (quarter) and 50c (half a dollar).
Notes (bills) – $1, $5, $10, $20, $50 and $100.
Be careful what you hand over and receive, because all the notes are the same colour. See **Money**.

Customs Allowances:

Duty Free Into:	Cigarettes	or	Cigars	or	Tobacco	Spirits	or	Wine
USA	200		50		4.4 lb	1*l*		1*l*
UK	200		50		250 g	1*l*		2*l*

Dates: The notation for dates is different in the USA, e.g. 3rd February 1994 would be abbreviated to 2.3.94 (as opposed to 3.2.94).

Disabled People: In general Florida is very accessible to wheelchair users. WDW is particularly good, with most attractions easily accessible. A free booklet, *A Guidebook for Guests with Disabilities*, is available from Walt Disney World, Box 10000, Lake Buena Vista, FL32830, tel: 407-5607090.
Most modern hotels have the latest up-to-date arrangements for access for people with disabilities, and there are parking bays assigned to disabled drivers outside every restaurant and shopping mall. For more information, get the *Florida Services Directory for the Physically Challenged Traveller* from the Florida Division of Tourism (see **Tourist Information**). See **Health**.

Drinks: The water in Florida is perfectly safe to drink, albeit heavily chlorinated in the Orlando area. Despite Florida's being one of the world's major citrus-growing areas, fruit juices are neither cheap nor readily available at refreshment stands, as you would expect. If you don't like over-iced colas and lemonades (with a hint of chlorine), take your own drinks to theme parks (but note that some do not allow this). Mineral water is common in bars and restaurants but varies considerably in price (from $1 3). American beer, which usually means Michelob or Budweiser, is, by general consent, weak and bland compared to European lagers. Served ice-cold, however, it is perfect for cooling off without getting drunk. European and Californian wines are on offer at most restaurants but usually start at around $12. There is often a choice of house wines and these are usually good value at around $5 per half-litre carafe. Cocktails are served almost everywhere and some people drink them with their meal, instead of wine. An important point to

remember is that the legal minimum age for drinking alcohol in Florida is 21, and this is strictly enforced (if you're under 30, have your passport with you and photographic ID when you go into a bar). American coffee is made weaker than the usual British brew but is quite drinkable and, with a meal, your cup is refilled free of charge. Try the thick, dark Cuban coffee in Miami's Little Havana (see **Miami**). Tea is an accepted American drink (always made with a tea bag) and is often drunk iced, with a meal.

Driving: North America drives on the right-hand side of the road. The speed limit is usually 30 mph in built-up areas and 55-65 mph on motorways (freeways/highways). Don't break the speed limits as Highway Patrol (see **Police**) are ever-present. A turnpike is a freeway with toll booths. For example, Boca Raton to Orlando Airport costs $9.10 in tolls. Bridges also are often tolled up to $3. You don't need the correct change but it will get you through the tolls faster. Expressways are quick routes into big cities and exits from these are sometimes from the fast (left-hand) lane. Interstate highways (marked 'I-' followed by a number) are the fastest routes. Try to avoid I-95 in the Miami/Fort Lauderdale area during rush hours. Note that Americans overtake on the inside as well as the outside lanes. In general, driving is much slower than in Britain and therefore helps you to adjust to the wrong side of the road quite easily. You must always carry your driving licence with you in case you are stopped. It is compulsory for children under five to sit in a special child seat or restraint; your car hire firm will rent you one. The law on front seat belts applies as in the UK. Traffic lights, generally slung high overhead, usually change from red straight to green; a constant flashing amber means proceed with caution and a flashing red means stop. You may ignore a red light if you are turning right, as long as your way is clear and there is no instruction to the contrary. If you see a (yellow) school bus loading or unloading and its lights are flashing, then you must stop, even if you are on the opposite side of the road. See **Accidents & Breakdowns**, **Crime & Theft**, **Parking**, **Petrol**.

Drugs: All drugs are illegal and there are severe penalties for offenders. Contact your consulate (see **A-Z**) if you are arrested for a drugs-related offence.

Eating Out: Cities and resorts have whole streets, courtyards or parts of malls dedicated to eating out. Isolated restaurants are a rarity. Food courts at shopping and entertainment centres often offer the best fast food, with many stalls selling ethnic foods (as well as burgers 'n' fries) around a central common-seating area. Small, quality chains (for example, Denny's or Bennigan's) are common, as are McDonald's, Pizza Hut and so on. These generally offer drive-in facilities on the outskirts of towns and cities. Expect high-quality service that puts the UK restaurant industry to shame. Orlando is chock-a-block with family-orientated restaurants, while Miami has a superb selection of ethnic cuisine.

Fort Lauderdale and Boca Raton boast some of Florida's poshest restaurants. See **MIAMI-RESTAURANTS 1 & 2**, **ORLANDO-RESTAURANTS**.

Electricity: 110-115 V. Small two-pin plugs are used. Adaptors are available in Florida and at airports. Establish before leaving whether your appliances will need a voltage transformer (although travel appliances often have a dual-voltage switch).

Emergency Numbers:

Police, Fire, Ambulance	911
Medical treatment	See **Health**

Events: Florida loves a festival and nowhere more so than Miami, where there is some sort of event going on almost every week. See the local press and what's-on publications for details (see **Newspapers**, **What's On**);. The following are major annual events.

January: Art Deco Weekend, Miami Beach.

February: Speed Weeks, car racing at Daytona; Big Orange Music Festival, free open-air concerts in Miami; Miami Grand Prix, Downtown, Miami; Gasparilla Festival, Tampa, month-long festivities.

Late February-early March: Miami Carnaval, eight to ten days of Latin festivities in Little Havana.

March: Medieval Fair, Sarasota, jousting, human chess and more.

April: Arts and Crafts Fair, St. Augustine.

Late April-early May: Conch Republic celebrations, Key West.

June: Coconut Grove Goombay Festival, Miami, a celebration of Bahamian culture.

Late June-early July (and early February): Silver Spurs Rodeo, Kissimmee, near Orlando.

July: Hemingway Days Festival, Key West; *4:* Independence Day celebrations, Miami Beach.

September: Festival Miami, three weeks of performing and visual arts; Oktoberfest (in September), Church Street Station, Orlando.

31 October: Hallowe'en celebrations at Key West (Fantasy Fest), Disney Village and Church Street Station, Orlando; Guavawe'en, Tampa, Latin-style Hallowe'en.

November: Florida Seafood Festival, Apalachicola.
Mid-November: Light Up Orlando, Downtown street party.
Mid-December: WDW Christmas Parade, Magic Kingdom.
Late December-January: Orange Bowl Festival, Miami.

Food: The native Florida menu is based on seafood.
Fish you may not be familiar with include yellowtail,
pompano, grouper, scrod and dolphin (a fish which is
completely different from the performing mammal variety!). Shellfish favourites are Maine lobster, crawfish
(Florida lobster), various kinds of crab (including stone
crabs, of which just the claws are eaten), oysters and
clams (often eaten raw in 'raw bars') and conch (pronounced 'conk'), which is a delicate-flavoured mollusc
speciality of the Keys. Virtually every type of cuisine is
served in Florida but the main types and some typical
dishes and terms are as follows:

American: The steak is king. A New York Strip is sirloin, and a prime-rib steak is very similar to roast beef.
Caesar salad is crispy romaine lettuce, croutons,
anchovies and Parmesan cheese plus a vinaigrette
dressing. Mesquite refers to the type of wood used
when barbecuing.
New American: This is an expensive hybrid of traditional American and French *nouvelle cuisine*, often
very rich and combining fruit sauces with meat dishes.
Cajun/Creole/Louisiana: Spicy sauces and blackened
meats (from a mixture of spices, not burning!) characterize this cuisine. Jambalaya is a paella-like dish of
seafood (often prawns or shrimps), sausage or ham,
perhaps chicken, and rice.
Cuban/Spanish: This is found mostly in Little Havana, Miami (see **A-Z**)
and in Ybor City in Tampa (see **A-Z**). Spanish-based dishes include
picadillo (marinated ground beef with olives, peppers, onions and
raisins, in a tomato sauce) and favourites such as paella and *arroz con
pollo* (chicken cooked in wine and spices, served with yellow rice).

Plantains and black beans are common accompaniments. When it states on the menu that the entreé comes with salad, the salad is usually served beforehand, as an extra course (although you can ask for it to be served altogether). In general, portions are large, with some restaurants actually expecting you to request a doggy bag. However, it is normally quite acceptable for two people to share one dessert or appetizer. The choice of desserts is often unadventurous – it's usually either cheesecake or Key lime pie (a frequently overrated, over-sweet relative of lemon meringue pie). See **MIAMI-RESTAURANTS 1 & 2**, **ORLANDO-RESTAURANTS**, **Eating Out**.

Health: The standard of medical care in Florida is high but so are the bills. Make sure you take out adequate health insurance before leaving home. Because of Florida's proximity to the equator it is easy to get badly burned while sunbathing, even in winter. Build up your tan slowly, using high protection-factor (15+) lotions. If you are visiting the Everglades in summer, you will need mosquito repellent. Beware of jellyfish and Portuguese men-of-war (look for warning notices on supervised beaches) which can sting even out of the water. Apply vinegar or urine if you are stung.
Medical treatment:
Orlando – Sandlake Hospital, 9400 Turkey Lake Rd, tel: 407-3518500.
Miami – Jackson Memorial Hospital, 1611 NW 12th Ave,
tel: 305-5857200.
Fort Lauderdale – North Beach Hospital, N Ocean Bd (A1A),
tel: 305-5653381.
See **Chemists**, **Insurance**.

Insurance: You should take out adequate travel insurance covering you against theft and loss of property and money, as well as medical expenses. Your travel agent should be able to recommend a suitable policy. See **Car Hire**, **Crime & Theft**, **Health**.

Laundries: Your hotel will probably offer a laundry and dry-cleaning service or a self-service Laundromat. These cost around $2 per load and $1.50 for drying.

Lost Property: If you lose something on Miami public transport, tel: 305-6386700. For WDW's lost and found service, tel: 407-8244245.

Markets: In the European sense of the word, markets are a rarity in Florida. Orlando's Farmers' Market, next to Church Street Station,

features freshly-baked goods, produce and flowers, plus live music (0730-1300 daily), and Coconut Grove Farmers' Market, Commodore Plaza, Coconut Grove, Miami sells ethnic foods, plants, craft items, jewellery and clothing while musicians play (0800-1500 Sat.). Ask at local tourist information centres for details of the nearest flea market. The world's largest indoor flea market is staged three or four times a year at Miami Beach, tel: 305-6519530 for details. Regular markets are held at Hollywood greyhound track (between Miami and Fort Lauderdale) 0800-1500 Sat. and Sun., and at NW 42nd Ave, New Hialeah, Miami Springs, tel: 305-6888080 for details. See **MIAMI-SHOPPING**, **ORLANDO-SHOPPING**, **Shopping**.

Money: Take US-dollar traveller's cheques with you to avoid having to go to the bank or exchange. These are accepted as currency virtually anywhere that handles a reasonable amount of cash, and as long as your purchase is reasonable, i.e. don't expect to buy a newspaper with a $100 traveller's cheque! You will be given change back in dollars with no transaction charge. If you want dollars for a small purchase then your hotel should be able to oblige free of charge. All major credit cards are readily accepted at hotels, restaurants, shops and by car hire firms. The latter will require a significant advance deposit in respect of hire charges, so if you are hiring a car a credit card is essential. See **Currency**, **Opening Times**.

Music: Miami has several major concert venues and whatever your taste in music you will find it here. Orlando is more limited but nevertheless still hosts big names, sometimes at a fraction of the price you would pay in Britain (expect to pay $25-35). Live rock, blues, jazz and reggae are all common in Miami bars and hotel nightspots, and if your tastes are Latin, then Little Havana (see **Miami**) will oblige. Tampa and Sarasota (something of a Mecca for those seeking high culture) have well known performing-arts centres offering opera, ballet and concerts. See **MIAMI-NIGHTLIFE 1 & 2, ORLANDO-NIGHTLIFE, What's On**.

Newspapers: The *Orlando Sentinel*, *Miami Herald* and *Tampa Tribune* are the area's main papers and they carry all entertainment listings. It is difficult to get British papers in Florida. In Miami, go to Frenchy's News, Commodore Plaza, Coconut Grove, Joe's News, 1549 Sunset Drive, South Dade or Barry's News, 7436 Collins Ave, North Miami Beach. In Orlando you can read, but not take away, the latest paper at Streets of London restaurant/pub, Old Town, Kissimmee. Ask at your hotel for local stockists. See **What's On**.

Nightlife: Miami boasts virtually every type of nightlife you can think of. Orlando and WDW are, by comparison, tame and family-orientated. However, with the recent additions of Church Street Station and Pleasure Island, there is something for all ages and tastes. Tampa's Ybor City offers the liveliest scene on the west coast. In the Panhandle, Panama City Beach has raucous discos that get swamped by US students, particularly in March. See **MIAMI-NIGHTLIFE 1 & 2, ORLANDO-NIGHTLIFE**.

Opening Times: In general:
Banks – 0900-1500 Mon.-Fri. (Drive-in banks 0900-1800 Mon.-Fri.). Some banks may open Sat. am.
Chemists – 0800/0900-2100/2400 Mon.-Sat. Many chemists also open on Sun.
Post Offices – 0830-1700 Mon.-Fri., 0830-1230 Sat.
Shopping Malls – 1000-2100 Mon.-Sat., 1200-1730 Sun.
Shops – 0930-1730 Mon.-Sat.
Museums – Times vary but most close Mon.

Orientation: The Florida Official Transportation Map (free) is the best to use for travel around the state. It also has good overview maps of all the cities you are likely to visit. However, such is the geographical size of centres such as Miami, Jacksonville, Tampa and Orlando that it is vital to get thorough directions to your first port of call. Rand McNally publishes detailed maps (available in the UK) but more useful are maps published by local convention and visitor bureaux.

Most cities are laid out on a grid pattern, with streets running east-west and avenues north-south. These street names have been abbreviated throughout the guide for ease of reference, so that, for example, South West 8th Street reads SW 8th St, North Mills Avenue reads N Mills Ave, and so on. All street names are marked at each intersection to help you navigate in town.

Before you set out on the freeway, find out the road number of your turn-off. It is quite possible that no names or districts will be given on the sign.

Most major roads have at least one name and number and you will almost certainly be using the following:
Fort Lauderdale/Miami/Florida Keys area – US/Highway 1 = Dixie Highway; Miami – US/Highway 41 = SW 8th St = Calle Ocho = Tamiami Trail; Orlando – US/Highway 192 = Irlo Bronson Memorial Highway; US/Highway 17-92-441 = South Orange Blossom Trail. The Florida Keys have Mile Markers running down the length of US/Highway 1. Miami, St. Augustine, Key West and other cities and resorts have trolley tours, which are a good way to get your bearings. The Metromover automatic train is the best way to see the Downtown district of Miami (see **A-Z**).

Parking: America is a car-dominated culture. As a result, stringent parking restrictions can be found everywhere. Meters take 25c coins. It is illegal to park within 10 ft of a fire hydrant and you could be towed away if you do. Recovery will cost at least $50. There is parking avail-ability in Downtown city areas, costing from $5 per day. Valet parking is common at larger hotels and posher restaurants (see **Crime & Theft**). It usually costs at least $4, sometimes much more. Most attractions, other than theme parks, provide free car parking. See **Driving**.

Passports & Customs: A valid passport is necessary, but no visa is required for stays not exceeding 90 days, and provided you have a return ticket. If you intend leaving the USA and re-entering (excluding a Bahamas day trip), you should enquire about a visa at the US embassy in London, tel: 071-4996846. See **Customs Allowances**.

Petrol: Known as 'gas' in the US. One US gallon equals 0.83 of a UK Imperial gallon and costs around $1.20. All hire cars run on unleaded. Some filling stations close in the evenings and on Sun. Others may require you to pay before you fill up. There is no need to tip attendants as attended stations are more expensive to compensate. See **Driving**.

Police: City Police control the city while Highway Patrol (State Troopers) patrol the highway. Don't be afraid to approach an officer for assistance, as they are usually courteous and helpful. In an emergency, tel: 911. See **Crime & Theft**.

Post Offices: Ask at your hotel to find out where the nearest sub-post office is. WDW's post office in Main St in the Magic Kingdom opens daily. It costs 40c to send a postcard to the UK (50c for a letter). Books of stamps are available almost everywhere, even the supermarket, but if you want just one or two stamps you will have to go to a post office. You can get stamps out of hours from dispensing machines in the post office lobby. See **Opening Times**.

Public Holidays: 1 Jan.; 3rd Mon. in Jan. (Martin Luther King Day); 3rd Mon. in Feb. (Washington's Birthday); last Mon. in May (Memorial Day); 4 July (Independence Day); 1st Mon. in Sep. (Labor Day); 2nd Mon. in Oct. (Columbus Day); 11 Nov. (Veterans' Day); 4th Thu. in Nov. (Thanksgiving Day); 25 Dec. Most shops are closed on New Year's Day, Thanksgiving Day and Christmas Day.

Railways: For information on rail travel in Florida, contact Destination Marketing Ltd, 2 Cinnamon Row, Plantation Wharf, York Place, London SW11 3TW, tel: 071-9785222. They can provide Amtrak (the American national railroad) timetables and 15- or 30-day regional rail passes such as the Coastal Pass and the Eastern Pass, both of which cover Florida. The cheapest is a 15-day Eastern Pass from $158. In the US, for information, tel: 1-800-USARAIL.

Religious Services: See the local Sat. newspaper for details of Sun. services. Look up 'Churches' for listings in *Yellow Pages*. Also, hotels have information on religious services.

Shopping: This is a serious American pastime and some malls have, literally, elevated it to an art form. Miami's Mayfair Shops in the Grove is one of the best examples, and the attractive Bal Harbor mall at Collins Ave is another. If you prefer fashionable, European-style street shopping, Orlando's Winter Park, Fort Lauderdale's Las Olas Bd, Palm Beach's Worth Ave, Boca Raton's Mizner Park and Naples' 3rd St S and 5th Ave S won't disappoint. At the other end of the price range is International Drive, Orlando, where discounts are the order of the day. WDW has themed shops to fit every child's fantasy, and Epcot has exotic shops and emporia from 11 countries. In Miami, don't miss the small shops in Coconut Grove (crafts) and around Red Rd and Sunset Drive in South Dade. Bayside Marketplace and the Disney Village Marketplace are great for souvenirs, and visit SW 8th St (Calle Ocho) for Cuban and Spanish wares. See MIAMI-SHOPPING, ORLANDO-SHOPPING, **Best Buys**, **Markets**, **Opening Times**.

Smoking: The only laws on smoking in public places apply on public transport, and smoking is prohibited inside most attractions. Most cinemas and restaurants allow smoking only in designated areas.

Sports: *Participatory sports:* There are more golf courses in Florida (over 1100) than any other state in the US: ask for the *Official Florida Golf Guide* from the Florida Division of Tourism in Tallahassee (see **Tourist Information**). Many of the larger resort complexes not only have tennis courts but even resident pros. Jogging is so popular that some hotels even detail running routes. Roller blading is the present exercise craze to hit the States: ask at your hotel for details on where to hire equipment.
Spectator sports:
American football – Miami Dolphins play (Sep.-Dec.) at the Joe Robbie

Stadium, NW 199th St, tel: 305-6205000; Tampa Bay Buccaneers play at Tampa Stadium, 4201 N Dale Mabry Highway, tel: 1-800-2820683. Tickets $18-30.

Baseball – Since April 1993 Florida has had its own major league baseball team. The Florida Marlins play (April-Oct.) at Miami's Joe Robbie Stadium, NW 199th St, tel: 305-6205000 ($4-13). In Mar. and April the country's premier teams train in stadiums across the state in the Grapefruit League ($4-13). Ask locally for details.

Basketball – Orlando Magic play at the Orlando Arena, tel: 407-649-BALL (up to $25). Miami Heat play (Nov.-May) at the Miami Arena, tel: 305-577-HEAT.

Hockey – Tampa Bay Lightning play Oct.-April ($12-50), tel: 813-2298800.

Horse racing – Calder Racecourse, NW 27th Ave, Miami, tel: 305-6251311 (grandstand $2, clubhouse $4). Hialeah Park, E 2nd Ave and 32nd St, Hialeah, Miami, tel: 305-8855800 (grandstand $2, clubhouse $4); beautiful landscaped course complete with 600 flamingos, worth a visit at any time (daily tours, free out of season, 1000-1600 Mon.-Sat.). Tampa Bay Downs, 11225 Race Track Road, tel: 813-8554401 (grandstand $1.50, clubhouse $3). Season runs Dec.-April.

Jai Alai (see **A-Z**) – Orlando Seminole Jai Alai, Fern Park, north of Orlando. 1900 Mon.-Sat., May-Jan. Tel: 407-3319191 for days of 1200 games ($1 general admission, $2 reserved seating); Miami Jai Alai Fronton, NW 37th Ave, 1915-2400 Mon.-Sat., 1200-1700 Mon., Wed. & Sat. (mid May-mid Sep., late Nov.-late April), tel: 305-6336400 for seat and dining reservations ($1 general admission, $5 clubhouse); Tampa Jai Alai, 5125 S Dale Mabry at Gandy Bd, tel: 813-8371411 ($1 general admission, $3-4 clubhouse).

See **Water Sports**.

Taxis: A cab should be licensed and metered (it won't necessarily be yellow), and carry an illuminated roof sign to indicate when it is for hire. Many cabs have their rates marked on the outside of their doors. Orlando rates are $2.25 for the first mile and $1.30 for each additional mile. Miami rates are $1.40 per mile. Night rates are higher. For sample fares from the airport, see **Airports**. See **Tipping**.

Telephones & Telegrams: Long-distance and international calls from hotels are extremely expensive. There are public telephones on street corners, in restaurants, bars, shopping malls, etc. Put a 25c coin in the slot, wait for the tone, then dial. If your call is over 25c the operator will advise you on how much to put in. To call long distance within the same area code dial 1 before the number; to call outside the area code dial 1 plus the area code plus the number. You can make international calls from most payphones. To call the UK, tel: 01144 then the STD code, less the first 0, and then the number. Telephones have letters alongside the numbers on the dial or keys and some services give the letters instead of numbers, as they are easier to remember, e.g. 800-WDISNEY. All numbers prefixed 800 are free but may only be used inside the USA or a particular state (those appearing in this guide may only be used in Florida). Calls are cheaper at weekends and in the evening. See **Emergency Numbers**.

Television & Radio: Virtually every hotel room has a television on which you can watch from 10 to 40 different channels. Most of them heavily feature news and sport. There are dozens of AM and FM radio stations to choose from, although many are very similar, playing adult-orientated rock (AOR).

Time Difference: Most of Florida is 5 hr behind GMT. Parts of the northwest, such as Pensacola, are 6 hr behind GMT.

Tipping: Waiting staff rely on tips for most of their salary and they will soon remind you of this if you don't leave the customary 15% on the table (though check to see if the bill includes service). Taxi drivers, tour guides and hairdressers should also be tipped 15%. Porters expect 50c-$1 for each bag carried and you should leave $3-5 per week for the hotel maid. See **Petrol**.

Toilets: Rest rooms. These can be found in all public places such as museums, stations, shopping malls and so on. They are usually unattended but are of a high standard and free of charge.

Tourist Information: *In the UK:* For a Florida vacation pack send a £2 cheque or postal order to ABC/See Florida, PO Box 35, Abingdon, Oxon, OX14 4SF. For WDW, write to ABC/Walt Disney Attractions, PO Box 35, Abingdon, Oxon, OX14 4TB. Orlando Convention and Visitor Bureau (CVB) has an office at 18-24 Westbourne Grove, London W2 5RH, tel: 071-2438072.
In Florida: Contact the Florida Division of Tourism, Visitor Enquiries, 126 W Van Buren St, Tallahassee, FL 32399-2000, tel: 904-4871462. For WDW, contact WDW Guest Information, PO Box 10040, Lake Buena Vista, FL 32830-0040, tel: 407-8244321. Each city or region has its own CVB. Main ones include: Orlando/Orange County CVB, 7208 Sand Lake Rd, Suite 300, Orlando, FL 32819, tel: 407-3635872; Greater Miami CVB, 701 Brickell Ave, Suite 2700, Miami, FL 33131,

tel: 305-5393000; Florida Keys and Key West CVB, PO Box 866, Key West, FL 33041-0866, tel: 305-2862228; Tampa/Hillsborough CVB, 111 Madison St, Suite 1010, Tampa, FL 33602-4706, tel: 813-2231111.
For information on the ground, in Miami visit Miami Beach Visitor Information at 1920 Meridian Ave, tel: 305-6721270, or Bayside Marketplace Visitor Information, tel: 305-5392982. In Orlando, the information centre at International Drive, tel: 407-3635872, is stuffed with information leaflets and discounts, but staff could be more helpful. Expect each resort to have a visitor centre, which will sometimes be in the CVB building, or in a kiosk by the beach.

Tours: The following tours are available in the Orlando area: Balloon – Several tours are available (enquire at the visitor centre – see

Key West

Tourist Information), the best-known being from Church Street Station. The trip departs at dawn and the cost of around $160 per person includes a champagne brunch and evening admission to Church Street Station. For details, tel: 407-841-UPUP.

Boat – 'Rivership Grand Romance' on the St. John's River is a peaceful dinner or lunch cruise through a tropical landscape. Lunchtime cruises 1100, dinner-dance cruises 1930-2300. N Palmetto Ave, Sanford, tel: 1-800-4237401.

Helicopter – Falcon Helicopters will fly you over Orlando and WDW (Disney tour $75, child $40), tel: 407-3526680.

Tours available from Miami/Fort Lauderdale/Florida Keys:

Boat – Nikko Gold Coast Cruisers make daily trips to Biscayne Bay and Millionaires' Row, Bayside Marketplace, Seaquarium, Vizcaya and Fort Lauderdale. $8 upwards, child under 13 $4.50 upwards. Contact Haulover Park Docks, Collins Ave, 108th St, North Miami Beach, tel: 305-9455461. There are also several tours, by various operators, departing regularly from Bayside Marketplace. See also the *Jungle Queen*, from Fort Lauderdale (see **FORT LAUDERDALE-ATTRACTIONS**).

Cruise ship – The most popular day trip from Miami is aboard the *SeaEscape*, sailing to the Bahamas. This trip costs $99, excluding port charges. See a travel agent, or tel: 1-800-8997797. *SeaEscape* also sails from Fort Lauderdale.

Rickshaw – A strapping young college type will haul you around Coconut Grove for a 10 min ride. $4 per person or a 20 min 'moonlight lovers' ride at $6 per person. Tours operate 2000-0200, from Main Highway, Coconut Grove, Miami.

Trolley tours – Old Town Trolley Tours conduct excellent tours of Miami and Key West. For the Miami tour buy your ticket at the kiosk at the entrance to Bayside Marketplace, $16, child $7. There are several stop-off points on the 90 min circular tour and you can reboard free all day. Trolleys pass every 30 min. Enjoy historic Key West with the same company at similar prices; tickets from Key West Welcome Center. Many other resorts and towns, such as St. Augustine, Tallahassee, Naples and Fort Myers, offer trolley tours too.

Walking – For tours of Miami's Art Deco district, see **Miami**.

Transport: Quite simply, you need a car when you are in Florida. Miami has a good public transport system, but this won't get you out to the best beaches or some of the sights. Unless you plan to confine yourself to WDW, it would be hard to get around in Orlando without wheels. Even in smaller resorts, the hotels, restaurants and beaches may be miles away from each other. Consider flying if you're planning to cover long distances. See **Airports**, **Buses**, **Railways**, **Taxis**.

Traveller's Cheques: See Money.

Water Sports: Whatever you fancy doing, above, below or on the water, you can do it in southern Florida. If you want to try jet-skiing, note there is a minimum age limit of 16 for hiring and 14 for operating, and you may have to leave a deposit. A jet-ski may be a single-operator stand-up machine (the trickiest to handle), or a Waverunner, a simpler, easier machine with a pillion seat. A Tandem Sports is larger and more stable than a Waverunner. Rental fees should always include a life jacket and basic instructions on handling and regulations. Hobie Cats are catamarans and to hire these you must be qualified. Boogie Boards are like surfboards on which you lie instead of stand. The speciality of much of the Gold coast (the coastline between Palm Beach and Miami Beach) is diving, due to the rich reef and sea life. For deep-sea fishing (particularly a Keys speciality) you'll have to pay $25 per person for a half day on a party boat, $250-plus for a boat for a group of four.

Snorkelling costs about $20 for a 2 hr tour. To scuba dive, you will need to have a certificate, and a course in Florida costs around $350. A dive trip costs around $40 (plus $35 for full equipment hire). If you wish to just potter around on the water, almost all seaside resort centres have marinas where you can hire motorboats and sailing craft. For more information, ask for the *Florida Fishing and Boating Guide* and *Florida Boating and Diving Guide* from the Florida Division of Tourism at Tallahassee (see **Tourist Information**). See **Sports**.

What's On: The *Miami Herald*, *Orlando Sentinel* and *Tampa Tribune* have general lists for cinema, theatre, nightclubs and so on. In Orlando, get the 'Calendar' section of the Fri. *Sentinel*. The *Herald* also has a 'Things to Do' weekend supplement every Fri. The Fort Lauderdale equivalent is the *Sun-Sentinel*'s Fri. 'Showtime'. Miami also has free listings publications: *New Times*, a weekly news and arts paper; *Inside Miami*, a month-ly major-events broadsheet; and *Welcome to Miami and Beach*, a small weekly maga-zine. The distribution of these is rather erratic, but try your hotel lobby and look for them in bars and restaurants. See **Events**, **Newspapers**.

Youth Hostels: For information contact American Youth Hostels Florida, PO Box 533097, Orlando FL 32853, tel: 407-8727996. There are youth hostels in Miami, Miami Beach, Panama City, St. Augustine, Daytona Beach, Key West and St. Petersburg, and two in Orlando.

This edition published 1995 by Diamond Books
77–85 Fulham Palace Road, Hammersmith, London W6 8JB

Text: Fred Mawer and Paul Murphy
Photography: Reflex Worldwide Ltd, Upfront Photography (64-65),
Pictor International (15 bottom, 70-71),
Tony Stone Worldwide (15 top, 99),
Travel Images (14, 75), Comstock (100-101)
Electronic Cartography: Susan Harvey Design and Morton Ward (1, 56)

First published as Miami/Orlando in 1990
Revised edition 1994
Copyright © HarperCollins*Publishers*

Printed in Italy

ISBN 0 261 66601 0